Exploring Alternative
Social Work Knowledge

Based on the Narratives of Practitioners from Sri Lanka

Group photo after the conference (2 November 2023)

Opening session

Editors

Masateru Higashida, Ph.D.

*Asian Research Institute for
International Social Work (ARIISW),
Shukutoku University,
Chiba, Japan*

M.T.R. Shamini Attanayake

*National Institute of Social
Development (NISD),
Seeduwa, Sri Lanka;*

*Sri Lanka Association of Professional
Social Workers (SLAPSW),
Pannipitiya, Sri Lanka*

Amarawansa Ranaweera

*Sri Lanka Association of Professional
Social Workers (SLAPSW),
Pannipitiya, Sri Lanka*

Muhammad Ashker, Ph.D.

*National Institute of Social
Development (NISD),
Seeduwa, Sri Lanka*

Exploring Alternative Social Work Knowledge

Based on the Narratives of Practitioners from Sri Lanka

Edited by

Masateru Higashida

Shamini Attanayake

Amarawansa Ranaweera

Muhammad Ashker

ARIISW-Shukutoku

Osaka Metropolitan University Press

Title: Exploring Alternative Social Work Knowledge: Based on the Narratives of Practitioners from Sri Lanka

Issued by the Asian Research Institute for International Social Work, Shukutoku University, 200 Daiganji-cho, Chuo-ku, Chiba 260-8701, Japan

Printed and bound by Ishikawa Special Express Binding Co. Ltd., 7-38 Ryuzoji-cho, Chuo-ku, Osaka 540-0014, Japan

Published by Osaka Metropolitan University Press, 1-1 Gakuen-cho, Naka-ku, Sakai, Osaka 599-8531, Japan

ISBN978-4-909933-76-8

This study was supported by JSPS KAKENHI Grant Nos. JP21K13477, JP24K16556 and JP21KK0039. This book was printed and published with funding from the Asian Research Institute for International Social Work, Shukutoku University.

Endorsement

I am pleased to extend my wholehearted endorsement of this book. This remarkable work is a testament to the collaborative efforts of the National Institute of Social Development (NISD). Drawing on rich experiences and in-depth dialogues, this book encapsulates a wealth of knowledge poised to contribute significantly to advancing social work locally and globally.

The collaborative nature of this endeavour reflects a commitment to excellence, ensuring that the book's insights are comprehensive and deeply rooted in the realities faced by those on the front lines of social work.

As a representative of the NISD, I am particularly pleased to see that our shared commitment to fostering positive change is embodied by this book. The potential for further development is evident, making this book an invaluable asset for anyone involved in social work, from seasoned professionals to those newly embarking on this noble journey.

In conclusion, I wholeheartedly recommend this book to anyone seeking a nuanced and insightful exploration of social work practices. Its collaborative foundation, which is rooted in real-world experiences, positions it as a cornerstone for the ongoing development of social work.

Dr H.W. Raveendra Kumara
Director General
National Institute of Social Development (NISD)

Endorsement

I am delighted to recommend this exceptional book, which is a commendable compilation of culturally relevant social work practices in Sri Lanka. The distinguishing characteristic of this book is that it draws extensively from the rich experiences of social workers. It skilfully weaves together a tapestry of insights, offering readers a nuanced and genuine understanding of social work in the country. It is a must-read for anyone interested in immersing themselves in a profound exploration of culturally relevant social work practices in a changing world.

Dr H.M.C.J. Herath
Director, Centre for Quality Assurance
Senior Lecturer, Department of Psychology and Counselling
Faculty of Health Sciences
The Open University of Sri Lanka

Preface

Numerous scholars worldwide argue the necessity of indigenous and local perspectives, although their actual practices are sometimes unclear. In this sense, exploring such local practical knowledge through dialogues among practitioners is crucial. In particular, these dialogues are expected to be practical and not necessarily academic. Thus, this book focuses on the knowledge and skills of social work practices in Sri Lanka, while considering its relationship with foreign and transnational knowledge. We hope this book will help develop social work education, training and practical theory in Sri Lanka, while having international implications for social work practices and research.

The editors of this book recognise that social work knowledge includes, or interrelates with, a broad and interdisciplinary set of information, evidence, theories, values and techniques, among others, that guide its practice (Barker, 1999; IFSW & IASSW, 2014). The areas of dominant or Western-rooted social work knowledge include social casework, group work, community organisation, social planning, social welfare administration, psychosocial assessment and intervention, research and advocacy (Barker, 1999). While this book strategically uses the term 'social work knowledge' in a broad sense—namely not limited to factual, dominant and/or scientific knowledge rooted in the West—it explores alternative knowledge, including local and indigenous knowledge(s) (IFSW & IASSW, 2014), based on practical field experiences.

The first editor of this book signed a research agreement with the Sri Lanka Association of Professional Social Workers (SLAPSW) after attaining due approval from the Research Ethics Committee of the Aomori University of Health and Welfare on 26 May 2021 (No. 21017), followed by a reconfirmation by the Research Ethics Committee of Shukutoku University in June 2022.

Following the kick-off meeting on 24 January 2023, the dialogues were co-organised and held at a joint conference on 2 November 2023 by the Asian Research Institute for International Social Work (ARIISW), the National Institute of Social Development (NISD) and SLAPSW. This book primarily comprises transcripts of selected presentations from this conference on social work's practical and subjective experiences, as a series of dialogues for the reciprocal exchange of social work knowledge titled Uncovering the Perspectives and Skills of Social Work Practices in the Sri Lankan Context. This preface outlines the book and establishes it in a global and a Sri Lankan context.

Global Context [1)]

The Global Definition of the Social Work Profession (hereafter referred to as the 'Global Definition') was adopted in 2014 and respects various types of local and indigenous knowledge, including the wisdom of indigenous peoples and ethnic minority groups. Such local and native knowledge can be considered traditionally and collectively inherited by people in specific contexts (cf. Mishima, 2016). While developing the Global Definition requires critical debate (Akimoto, 2015), concerns exist regarding the hegemony of colonialism and Western-centrism, especially in international discussions on indigenous erudition (Dominelli, 2012).

Scholars have explored culturally relevant social work practices and education (Gray & Coates, 2010), while academic discussions have focused on local and indigenous knowledge and indigenous and post-colonial social work (e.g. Rowe et al., 2015; Twikirize & Spitzer, 2019). Furthermore, there is a growing debate in the Asian context about the relationship between indigenous knowledge and social work. This debate encompasses various aspects, such as how community-based local knowledge not limited to indigenous peoples' wisdom can be described without the premise of Western-rooted professional social work (Akimoto et al., 2020). Notwithstanding whether social work is recognised as a profession in Asia, social workers in this region may not rely solely on local and indigenous knowledge. Instead, international norms are intertwined in various forms due to globalism, while the pluralism of awareness and experiences is assumed (Higashida, 2023a).

Given such complex contexts, this book adopts the multi-faceted perspective of international social work (Akimoto, 2004). Thus, international and mutually reciprocal exchanges represent the classical theme of social work

1) This section was edited for reprint based on previous research: Higashida, M., Attanayake, S., Ranaweera, A., Ashker, M. & Kumara, R. (2023). Dialogue for the reciprocal exchange of social work knowledge in Sri Lanka. Annual report of the Asian Research Institute for International Social Work, 7, 7–13. Chiba: Shukutoku University.

(Midgley, 2016). In particular, we consider various aspects, such as 'inside' and 'outside' positions and focus on the possibility that tacit knowledge can be discovered or created through dialogues among people in diverse positions (Higashida, 2023c).

More discussions are needed on the unique local and indigenous knowledge applied to social work practices and the interactions of such realisations with foreign knowledge. For example, a survey of an actual situation was conducted in the Asian context and a theoretical examination of the social work practices adopted by Buddhist monks and nuns was performed from the perspective of Buddhist social work (Akimoto, 2020; Higashida, 2024). In addition, we transcend specific religious frameworks to introduce a dialogue on how this issue can be elucidated according to the interrelationships between local and indigenous knowledge and the practices adopted by social workers (Higashida, 2023a). We argue that current research activities can explore alternative erudition and discourses that differ from the dominant discourses, if such practical dialogues can clarify the opportunities and challenges of social workers across borders.

Sri Lankan Social Work Context [2]

The Democratic Socialist Republic of Sri Lanka is a multi-ethnic, multi-religious country that has undergone several periods of colonisation under the Portuguese, Dutch and British before declaring independence as the Dominion of Ceylon in 1948 and adopting its current state name in 1978. More than 70% of its population is Sinhalese, followed by Sri Lankan Tamil, Sri Lankan Moor, Indian Tamil, Burgher, Malay, Sri Lankan Chetty, Bharatha and Vedda and others (Department of Census and Statistics, 2012).[3] As for their religious faith, most Sinhalese people are Theravada Buddhists, while others follow religions such as Christianity. Meanwhile, those from other ethnic backgrounds practice mainly Hinduism and Islam.

Sri Lankan traditional societies were largely founded on peasant

---

2) This section has been edited for reprint based on previous research: Higashida, M., Ranaweera, A. & Herath, C. (2022). Exploring social representations of social work in the Sri Lankan cultural context: A qualitative study. Sustainability, 14(23).

3) According to the Department of Census and Statistics, Sri Lanka, the 15th Census of Population and Housing will be conducted in 2023/2024.

agriculture, ideological norms and distinctive gender roles influenced by religious values and occupational caste systems (International Labour Organisation, 2020; Perera, 1991). During the past several decades, significant changes have occurred in the country's historical, political, socio-cultural and religious contexts, mainly due to the civil war (1983–2009), the 2004 Indian Ocean earthquake and tsunami and the recent economic crisis (Razick, 2017; Unnathi & Samaraweera, 2024; Uyangoda, 2005). Therefore, Sri Lanka's history of colonisation, its multi-ethnic and multi-religious contexts and its traditional (but changing) social system are likely interrelated with local and indigenous social work activities (Gray & Coates, 2010; Noyoo & Kleibl, 2019).

When foreign social welfare systems, such as the British model, were introduced, its interactions with Western-rooted approaches and stakeholders influenced Sri Lanka's social work education and training (Ranaweera, 2013). Social work education is headed by the School of Social Work at the National Institute of Social Development (NISD), whose predecessor was established in 1952 (Samaraweera, 2020; Shamila, 2020). Since its establishment, the School of Social Work has incorporated both Western and foreign social work theories[4] (Ranaweera, 2013), evident in the interactions and synergy between Sri Lankan social workers and international stakeholders. Moreover, some scholars have described how the development of social work education programmes involved international actors such as the United Nations, Canada and the NISD staff who completed their social work education abroad (Samaraweera, 2020; Shamila, 2020).

However, certain scholars have identified the challenges of applying Western-rooted theories to social work development in Sri Lanka due to its diverse socio-cultural contexts and fluctuating resources (Samaraweera, 2020; Shamila, 2020; Unnathi & Samaraweera, 2024). For example, a researcher indicated that introducing Western-rooted social work approaches in Sri Lankan society is inappropriate due to their different social and cultural norms, including mutual-help systems in communities and intra-family dynamics (Somananda, 2020). Therefore, social work education and practice development is argued to be relevant in the Sri Lankan context. In this regard,

---

4) For instance, Dr Dorothy Moses, the first principal of the Delhi School of Social Work at the University of Delhi, served as a consultant for the UNESCO programme, which aimed to develop social work education and training (Ranaweera, 2013).

some researchers have posited that even before the emergence of 'Western-rooted professional social work' in the country, Buddhist monks and nuns had already been participating in social work activities based on Buddhist principles (Akimoto, 2017, 2020; Wickramasinghe et al., 2020). Meanwhile, other researchers have recognised existing social work practices in the Sri Lankan context, including community mobilisation, spirituality and sustainable development perspectives, especially in case studies of government employees and workers from non-governmental organisation (NGO) (Higashida, 2016, 2023a). In summary, considering the development of social work education and practice in Sri Lanka, it is crucial to critically discuss the challenges, including controversial issues such as the relationship between indigenous knowledge and theories and practices rooted in Western culture in this era of globalisation (Higashida, 2023a).

Structure of the Book

As the editors, we are honoured to introduce this extensive exploration of social work practices in Sri Lanka in the context of global and transnational knowledge exchange. This book comprises 11 chapters, with three distinct parts, each delving into various aspects of social work and its relationship with both local and foreign perspectives.

Part I covers the first two chapters, providing a foundational understanding of our discussions. Chapter 1 addresses the importance and inherent challenges of sharing subjective experiences of social work practices. Meanwhile, Chapter 2 explores the invaluable role of volunteerism and altruism in shaping social work paradigms.

Moving into Part II, the exploration deepens with Chapters 3 through 9, highlighting specific experiences in community-based rehabilitation (Chapter 3), insights from the perspective of *Grama Niladhari*, namely, civil servant working at the village level (Chapter 4) and the crucial task of empowering parents for the future well-being of children with disabilities (Chapter 5). This section also explores the importance of cultural practices in fostering inter-ethnic understanding (Chapter 6) and emphasises youth empowerment through community development initiatives (Chapter 7). Furthermore, Part II examines the incorporation of social case work practices (Chapter 8), emphasising individual well-being through comprehensive support, while also delving into indigenous supervision practices that optimise fieldwork, as shared through reflective accounts (Chapter 9).

Lastly, Part III serves as a platform for critical discourse, encompassing Chapters 10 and 11. Chapter 10 delves into the rationale behind focusing on local and foreign knowledge in social work practice. Chapter 11 culminates in a collaborative exploration of alternative knowledge in social work practices through a dialogue. This dialogue contains a variety of points of view but suggests the potential of diverse discourses on social work in the Sri Lankan context.

This book bridges the rich tapestry of social work experiences in Sri Lanka and the broader global discourse, highlighting the exchange of knowledge, experiences and practices to advance the field. Each chapter offers a unique perspective, contributing to a holistic understanding of the intricate relationships between social work, culture and the global context. We recognise that the authors and speakers have presented several different views on social work, such as a sense of distance towards local/indigenous and foreign/Western knowledge. However, we include them because they are still relevant to our topic and discussion.

We hope that this compilation enriches our understanding of social work practices in Sri Lanka and inspires further collaborations and idea exchanges among practitioners, scholars and enthusiasts in the field globally and locally. The presenters and editors edited the content. We also thank all the presenters and participants at the conference.

On behalf of the editors, 1 April 2024
Dr Masateru Higashida
Asian Research Institute for International Social Work
Shukutoku University

Acknowledgements

(from the opening speech at the conference on 2 November 2023)

I am honoured to extend my warmest welcome to all the participants at this conference, which was co-organised by the National Institute of Social Development, the Sri Lanka Association of Professional Social Workers and the ARIISW. I truly hope you have come together to facilitate this important exchange of knowledge and ideas.

The theme of this joint conference, *Uncovering the Perspectives and Skills of Social Work Practices in the Sri Lankan Context,* resonates profoundly with certain values/viewpoints, including those of the ARIISW. The need for collaborative efforts, innovative solutions and shared understanding has never been greater in our rapidly evolving world. Therefore, this conference provides a vital platform for social work practitioners and scholars of diverse fields to engage in meaningful dialogues that can help shape a better future for all.

I would like to extend my gratitude to the organising committee, the speakers and each participant for their dedication in making this event possible. Your collective experiences and contributions will indeed enrich future discussions and inspire new avenues of social work practice and research. I encourage everyone to actively participate, exchange your insights and embrace the spirit of collaboration.

As I conclude this message, I would like to express my utmost confidence that this conference will be a resounding success. May your discussions be fruitful, interactions be enlightening and experiences be memorable.

Thank you again for your commitment to excellence and for participating in this remarkable journey. I look forward to hearing about the exciting developments and insights from this conference. We wish you all a productive and enriching experience.

Professor Noriko Totsuka
Director
Asian Research Institute for International Social Work
Shukutoku University

Chapter Contributors

Amarawansa Ranaweera, Sri Lanka Association of Professional Social Workers, Pannipitiya, Sri Lanka

Chandima Jayasena, Department of Social Work, Pondicherry University, India

E.A. Upeksha Piyumanthi, *Grama Niladhari*, Kandy, Sri Lanka

K.H. Chamara Kumarasinghe, Social Services Officer, Katana, Sri Lanka

Masateru Higashida, Asian Research Institute for International Social Work, Shukutoku University, Chiba, Japan

M.T.R. Shamini Attanayake, National Institute of Social Development, Seeduwa, Sri Lanka; Sri Lanka Association of Professional Social Workers, Pannipitiya, Sri Lanka

Muhammad Ashker, U., National Institute of Social Development, Sri Lanka

R.M.H. Yasintha Rathnayake, Independent Practitioner, Sri Lanka

Saroja P. Weththewa, Chief Social Services Officer, Anuradhapura, Sri Lanka

Tharindu Kasunpriya, The T.E.A. Project, Hanthana, Kandy, Sri Lanka

Varathagowry Vasudevan, National Institute of Social Development, Sri Lanka

Vivetha Gunaretnam, International Resource Development and Management, World Vision International, Sri Lanka

The affiliation status as of 2 November 2023.

Contents

PART III: DIALOGUE

Abbreviations

APASWE	Asian and Pacific Association for Social Work Education
ARIISW	Asian Research Institute for International Social Work
BSW	Bachelor of Social Work
CRPO	Child Rights Protection Officer
IASSW	International Association of Schools of Social Work
IFSW	International Federation of Social Workers
INGO	International Non-governmental Organisation
MOH	Medical Officers of Health
MSW	Master of Social Work
NGO	Non-governmental Organisation
NISD	National Institute of Social Development
SLAPSW	Sri Lanka Association of Professional Social Workers
SSO	Social Services Officer
UGC	University Grants Commission
UN	United Nations
UNICEF	United Nations Children's Fund
UNESCO	United Nations Educational, Scientific and Cultural Organisation

Location of Sri Lanka

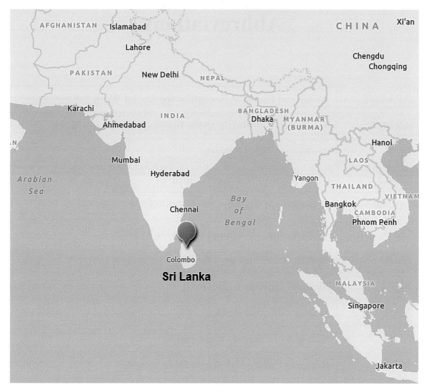

Note: Retrieved with the modification of the editors from ArcGIS online.

Map of Sri Lanka

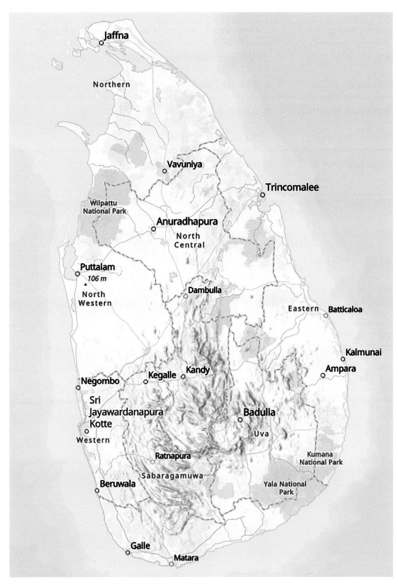

Note: Retrieved from ArcGIS online.

4

Basic Information on Sri Lanka

Country name	Democratic Socialist Republic of Sri Lanka
Capital	Sri Jayawardenepura Kotte
Total area	65,610.2 km^2
Population (estimated)[1]	About 22.1 million (2022)
Official languages	Sinhala and Tamil
Ethnic groups (2012)[2]	Sinhalese (74.9%) Sri Lankan Tamils (11.2%) Sri Lankan Moors (9.2%) Indian Tamils (4.2%) Others (0.5%)
Religions (2012)[2]	Buddhism (70.1%) Hindu (12.6%) Islam (9.7%) Christianity (7.6%)

Sources: 1. World Bank (https://data.worldbank.org/indicator/);
2. Department of Census and Statistics (http://www.statistics.gov.lk/)

Introduction: An Examination of the Past and Future Potential of Social Work Education in Sri Lanka

Muhammad Ashker, U.
School of Social Work, National Institute of Social Development

Editors' note: This book does not necessarily focus on official or professional social work education, but this introduction addresses its history and future potential to provide background information. The author draws on historical sources (National Archives of Sri Lanka, 1976, 1982, n.d.) to summarise the historical context of social work education in Sri Lanka.

The Origin of Professional Social Work Education

The history of the Institute of Social Work in Sri Lanka dates back to 1952 when it was established as a voluntary organisation. Over time, the institution has undergone many changes and it was renamed the Ceylon School of Social Work in 1964. It is currently a government institution that operates under the Ministry of Women, Child Affairs and Social Empowerment.

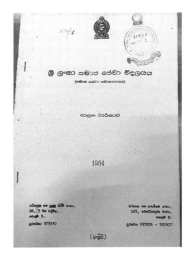

- 1952: The Institute of Social Work established as a voluntary organisation
- 1964: Renamed as the Ceylon School of Social Work, a government institution under the Ministry of Social Welfare
- 1972: Renamed the Sri Lanka School of Social Work.
- 1978: Introduction of a full-time two-year diploma programme in social work taught in local languages
- 1978: Curriculum development in consultation with leading educators under UN guidance

The institution was changed again in 1972, becoming the Sri Lanka School of Social Work. This name change was a clear indication of the school's commitment to providing education in the field of social work. In 1978, the school introduced a comprehensive two-year diploma programme in social work. Programme instruction was carried out in multiple local languages and curricular improvements were implemented according to the guidance provided by the United Nations. These strategic modifications represented significant milestones in the expansion of the professional social work education in Sri Lanka.

The Sri Lanka School of Social Work was initially a volunteer organisation focused on short training programmes for social workers. In 1964, the school was officially renamed the Ceylon School of Social Work. It later became a government institution under the Ministry of Social Welfare and in 1972, the Sri Lanka School of Social Work was established. A new Diploma in Social Work was introduced in 1978, offering a two-year programme taught in local languages. After the government took over in 1964, the school became part of the Department of Social Services. In 1978, a new curriculum was developed in consultation with leading educators at the UN. Faculty members were sent abroad for postgraduate training and the school expanded its activities to include research and publication.

Child Welfare Training by the School of Social Work

Since 1974, the Sri Lanka School of Social Work has been actively involved in providing child welfare training. In 1978, the school introduced a Diploma in Social Work specialising in child welfare. The school expanded its focus to include research and publications on child development, with a particular emphasis on providing comprehensive training programmes. The Sri Lankan/Canadian Social Work Linkage Project was started in 1983 as part of a partnership with the University of Toronto. This partnership played a vital role in developing the curriculum and field instruction.

The school has conducted training sessions for kindergarten staff in rural and urban areas and tea plantation areas. In addition, the school has organised seminars for in-home caregivers for children, parents, preschool and primary school teachers and social workers engaged in child welfare. To support the growth of individuals involved in child development activities, the school publishes literature in local languages, produces educational videos and develops other materials that can be used in the field.

An example can be seen in the translation and dissemination of 'The Child and His Development from Birth to Six Years Old', first published in Paris in 1976 under the auspices of UNESCO. The content released has shown significant advantages for social workers in child welfare and community services and novice social workers. The president of UNESCO authorised the translation of the book into Sinhala, with the support of the United Nations Children's Fund (UNICEF) headquarters in Sri Lanka.

- 1974: Sri Lanka School of Social Work actively involved in training social workers for child welfare activities
- 1978: Introduction of a diploma programme in social work for child welfare
- 1978: Expansion into research and publications related to child development.
- 1983: Launch of the Sri Lankan/Canadian Social Work Linkage Project with the University of Toronto, contributing to curriculum development and field instruction

Short-Term Training for Probation and Child Protection Officers

The Sri Lanka School of Social Work, founded in 1983, collaborated closely with the University of Toronto to improve its academic programmes. The primary objective of this collaboration was to improve the institution's academic offerings by developing curricula and providing field teaching. In 1979, the school oversaw a programme in which its teaching members were sent abroad to receive postgraduate education to ensure that they could obtain knowledge that would enable them to provide exceptional instruction in the field of social work.

The institution prioritises training probation and child protection officers, acknowledging the importance of comprehensive training for professional growth. The institute has introduced brief training programmes, including lecture materials, to adequately equip officers. These programmes help officers to carry out their responsibilities before receiving extensive training. This comprehensive approach guarantees that officers have the necessary information and abilities to perform their duties, thus improving the efficiency of probation and child protection services.

The institute also provides vocational courses that aim to equip students with the practical skills and knowledge needed in social work. Trainees, who usually receive extensive training before being assigned to a service station, receive lecture notes from a short-term training course to help them perform their tasks until they can receive extended training.

The faculty of the Sri Lankan School of Social Work consisted of seven instructors with postgraduate qualifications. In 1983, the school partnered with the University of Toronto to create a curriculum and provide Sri Lankan instructors with practical training in the field. The institution implemented a paraprofessional training curriculum specifically emphasising research and publication. To cope with the higher workload, faculty members were sent overseas to pursue advanced degrees in social work. In 1983, the Sri Lankan/Canadian

Social Work Linkage Project provided guidance to the faculty, which resulted in establishing a new degree programme. The school aims to offer a two-year diploma programme and in-service and pre-service training opportunities. Additionally, the school focuses on conducting research and publishing scholarship. However, the governmental administrative report emphasised the difficulties in providing housing and the need for a specialised facility. Despite limited financial resources, the institution organised an introductory training programme for probation and prison welfare officials. The future objectives of the school include the establishment of field centres, the implementation of a degree programme and the introduction of advanced certification courses.

Within the publishing domain, the school prioritises producing additional reading materials in the Sinhala language, as such resources are scarce. This effort involves producing translations and creating educational resources. The report concludes with financial statements that demonstrate the continuous efforts and ambitions of the Sri Lanka School of Social Work. However, during that period, schools were established based on a specific curriculum, including the following content, which laid the foundation for the degree programme in Sri Lanka.

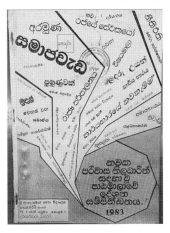

- To offer a two-year study course leading to a Diploma in Social Work.
- Conduct in-service, pre-service and on-the-job training programmes
- Engage in research, produce teaching materials and publish educational resources
- Introduce a Family Counselling Training Programme

Faculty Development and Collaborations:
- 1983: Collaboration with the University of Toronto for curriculum development and field instruction.
- Faculty Qualifications: Recognition of the need for faculty members to be well-qualified led to sending faculty members abroad to obtain postgraduate education

The Importance of Social Work Education in Sri Lanka

Social organising is a crucial aspect of social work that addresses the challenges individuals, families, groups and communities face. It also fosters social development through schools, hospitals and welfare centres. The complexity of society has increased because of rapid changes in society and global economic development, particularly in Asian, Latin American and African countries. Common fields of social work include medicine, psychiatry, education, rural communities, urban areas, rehabilitation, elder care work and child, family, disability, labour and youth and tribal welfare.

In Sri Lanka, social work fields operate to some extent with the participation of social workers; however, their involvement is not consistently planned or executed. Key issues resulting from ethnic conflict include breaches of the peace, disharmony, a lack of trust among community members, population displacement, broken families and psychological pressures faced by the armed forces. The roles of social workers in solving these problems have been deemed inadequate and their participation is noticeable.

Social workers must leverage their knowledge, vision and ethical perspectives to address major social problems while focusing on influencing stakeholders in the peace process, building confidence among the population, minimising psychological, physical and social problems caused by war and contributing to the resettlement and reestablishment of families affected by conflict. They must dedicate themselves to raising education standards, improving health, increasing income levels, providing employment, resettling individuals and re-establishing broken families.

Conceptual Development and Challenges in Social Work
1. Social work profession:
   - Role in society: Social work is crucial in resolving psychological, social and economic issues.
   - Involvement of social institutions: Social workers should become involved with institutions such as schools, hospitals and welfare centres.
2. Global demand for social work:
   - Increasing demand: There is a surge in demand in Asian, Latin American and African countries due to economic hardships.
   - Common fields: Various fields of social work are applicable globally.
3. Challenges in Sri Lanka:
   - Ethnic conflict: Challenges arose from ethnic conflict, including breaches of peace, population displacement, broken families and psychological pressures placed on the armed forces.
   - Role of social workers: The role of social workers is perceived inadequate in addressing these challenges.

4. Responsibilities of social workers:

   - Prompt action needed: There is an urgent need for social workers to leverage their knowledge, vision and ethical perspectives.
   - Focus areas: Peace processes; confidence-building; addressing psychological, physical and social problems caused by war; and the resettlement and reestablishment of affected families.
5. Training of social workers:
   - Importance of training: Emphasis on proper training to ensure effective participation in addressing societal challenges.

Faculty Development and Collaboration

The Department of Social Work underwent an overhaul and was officially renamed the National Institute of Social Development (NISD) according to the enactment of Parliament Act No. 41 of 1992. In 2003, the University of Colombo and the NISD signed a memorandum of understanding in response to the recommendation of the University Grants Commission (UGC) to partner with a local university to create a BSW programme.

In 2005, the Sri Lankan Government recognised the status of the NISD as a degree-awarding institution following the recommendation of the UGC. This declaration promoted higher education and allowed the institute to confer bachelor's degrees in social work. The order was published in the Gazette Extraordinary No. 1395/15 of 01 June 2005, under Section 25A of the Universities Act No. 16 of 1978. The Bachelor of Social Work (BSW) degree programme began in December 2005.

The UGC approved a master's degree programme in social work. To formalise this approval, the Sri Lankan Government rescinded the previous order from 2005 and declared the NISD as an institution that can award degrees. This allows the institute to offer BSW and Master of Social Work (MSW) degrees. The declaration was made under Section 25A of the Universities Act No. 16 of 1978 and was published in the Gazette Extraordinary No. 1557/7 on 07 July 2008.

The NISD is an established institution that provides a comprehensive MSW programme emphasising classroom-based teaching. The programme is designed for students interested in acquiring academic knowledge and skills in the field of social work. Provides a flexible course schedule. The institute offers a 1-year MSW degree programme with a comprehensive curriculum and a 2-year MSW programme emphasising research skills. The programme is tailored to accommodate the many needs of participants, whether they intend to work within their local communities or operate on a global scale. The institute's commitment to academic excellence is seen in its provision of social work education at all three academic levels. The BSW degree was established in 2005 and the master's degree programme was initiated in 2008. The institute's faculty, which consisted of seven instructors with postgraduate qualifications, demonstrated academic excellence. The Sri Lankan/Canadian Social Work Linkage Project, which began in 1983, achieved notable achievements in curriculum design. The institute provides an extensive range of programmes, including a two-year diploma programme for professionals already working in the field and those preparing to enter it. The programme focuses on research and academic publications. The institute intends to develop field centres, implement a degree programme and initiate advanced certification courses.

The NISD has undertaken significantly revised its BSW with specialisation in social work practice (e.g. school social work, medical and mental health and disaster management and disabilities studies) and MSW curricula. The last amendments were implemented in 2013 for BSW and in 2007/2008 for MSW. In particular, the MSW prospectus was renewed to incorporate one- and two-year programmes and additional specialisations such as social work with children and families, correctional social work, medical and mental health social work, geriatric social work and ecological/environmental social work. This amendment marks the introduction of prospectuses for both bachelor's and master's programmes for the first time in NISD's history.

In addition to these initiatives, NISD has established a Medical Care Unit and a Student Welfare Unit. Internal and external staff capacity development programmes have also been launched. Moreover, the institution encourages students to engage in extracurricular activities through societies and clubs focused on music, drama, sports and culture. Additionally, the institute has purchased new furniture for students and staff to improve the learning environment.

Several new programmes have been proposed to improve social work in Sri Lanka, including a *Diploma in Social Case Work and Case Management* for field-level officers employed in government and NGOs. In addition, a *Diploma in Social Work* programme is being introduced in regional centres at all three educational levels along with a specialised *Diploma in Industrial Social Work*. These initiatives aim to accelerate the professionalisation of social work by establishing a Social Work Council to monitor domain-related education and practice standards throughout the country.

NISD endeavours to foster knowledge dissemination and exchange by publishing its students' research findings and field experiences in local, regional and international journals. Furthermore, the institute prioritises integrating model villages and collaborative practices with multidisciplinary teams to emphasise holistic approaches to social welfare. It is developing partnerships with varied stakeholders, including field supervisors and government, local, regional and international agencies, to strengthen professional practices and promote effective service delivery. Therefore, these initiatives collectively signify a concerted effort to raise the standards and impact of social work in Sri Lanka.

PART I:
FRAMEWORK

Chapter 1: Significance and Challenges of Sharing Experiences in Social Work Practices

Amarawansa Ranaweera
Sri Lanka Association of Professional Social Workers (SLAPSW)

Abstract: The theme of this conference is *Uncovering the Perspectives and Skills of Social Work Practices in the Sri Lankan Context*. This indicates that social work perspectives and skills have not yet been adequately defined or understood in Sri Lanka, especially in the socio-cultural context. The conference's objective clearly states that the 'purpose of this conference is to exchange knowledge and skills in the practices of social work in Sri Lanka'. Furthermore, it states that 'many scholars worldwide argue the need for indigenous and local perspectives, even though their actual practices are sometimes unclear'. This statement is especially relevant to us. We have been discussing the issue of defining social work in the Sri Lankan context for a considerable period; however, we have yet to reach a consensus. Therefore, this initiative is a remarkable step towards studying social work in this country.

Keywords: Social work practices, Knowledge sharing, Sharing experiences, Challenges

Social Work in the Sri Lankan Context

Compassion is deeply rooted in human nature and has a biological basis in both the brain and the body (Stellar & Keltner, 2014). Hence, humans can communicate compassion through facial gestures and touch and such displays can serve vital social functions. Furthermore, this nature can also be observed among the Sri Lankan people. For example, helping others has been a trait of Sri Lankan society since ancient times. This characteristic is further promoted by the fundamental principles of the religious beliefs in the country, which include compassion, kindness, mutual help, interdependency and self-reliance. Meanwhile, most of the country's religious organisations help those in need by offering materials, money and counselling. Can we consider these services as social work?

Sri Lanka is a predominantly agricultural and rural country. In this society, kinship, family relationships and community feelings are strong and are the primary informal resources for providing help for those in distress. The report of the Commission on Social Services, popularly known as the *Jennings Report,* published in 1946, stated the following about the social context of Ceylon: Mutual assistance is still given more readily and on a larger scale than in the case in most industrialised societies and it provides a 'cushion' against distress, which renders less necessity the intervention of the organised community. This social context remains prevalent in the country, with some changes after its independence. Meanwhile, the family, relatives and community share a major part of the responsibility of providing care for people who are chronically sick, people with disabilities, the elderly, children, the unemployed and the poor, among others. Can these informal services be considered social work?

The state's provision of services to those in need was minimal during the colonial period. However, after independence, such services were offered by the governmental sectors, such as social services, probation and childcare departments. Currently, various ministries and departments provide such social services through a cadre of officers sent to various areas of the country. These services are called 'social services' or 'social welfare services', raising the next question: Can these services be considered social work?

There is no synonymous term for the English term 'social work' in Sri Lanka. Instead, various terms are used, including *samaaja wada, samaaja karya, samaaja vruthavedaya* and *samuha pani.* This indicates that social work is a foreign term for Sri Lankans. Furthermore, they are more familiar with the term 'social services' than social work, while implying a similarity to charity work. As stated above, even government and non-government entities refer to this support as 'social services'.

Many social workers tend to quote international definitions, such as the Global Definition of the Social Work Profession (IFSW & IASSW, 2014) and other well-established international social work professional organisations to explain the meaning of social work. Accordingly, social work is a practice-based profession and academic discipline in which social work's values, principles, skills and knowledge are directed towards helping people. However, even more than half a century after the introduction of 'modern' social work in Sri Lanka, social work has not been officially recognised as a profession. This lack of recognition by the state as a profession, the absence of a code of ethics and the unfavourable structures for social work professional practice in organisations indicate that Sri Lankan social work does not align with international definitions. Again, social work is an alienated profession in Sri Lanka. In other words, it is necessary to understand the context in which social work has developed in Western industrialised countries.

Social work is a product of Western industrialised economies developed in the late 19th century. It emerged based on their idealistic belief that the state can overcome social problems by using science and knowledge (Offer, 2006). Therefore, in most countries, it is part of state services and claims rational evidence as the basis of its practice. Especially in wealthy Western countries, social work is substantially part of the state and an organised public welfare provision (Payne & Askeland, 2016).

How do we Find an Answer to this Issue?

To date, no systematic approach (e.g. research, discussions and academic inputs) to determining the meaning of social work or social work practice in Sri Lanka has existed. Thus, we must examine the history of people helping others in society, investigate values, beliefs and norms concerning providing help for those in need, conduct research on the organised provision of welfare services for them and develop dialogues among social work practitioners, to obtain a better understanding of social work practice.

Significance of Sharing Experiences

Developing skills without practice is impossible. For instance, a person should practice driving a car to develop their skills: the person learns how to start, move, turn and stop by following the instructions given by an instructor. The longer the period of time to do it, the higher their skills will be. In this case, experience comes with time, exposure and practice. Discussing one's experience will also help others improve their experiences. As for social work skills, they combine hard and soft skills, both of which are based on specific knowledge and values. In other words, they are considered competencies.

Sharing experiences, which is a learning process, has been significant in social work practice and education. According to the experiential learning theory of Kolb et al. (2014), concrete experiences, reflective observations, abstract conceptualisations and active experimentation form a cycle that transforms into effective learning. First, social work interventions are concrete experiences, after which a social worker considers what went well (or wrong) through reflective observations. Subsequently, a social worker develops new knowledge through abstract conceptualisation. Fellow social workers can relate their own experiences, develop abstract conceptualisation and experiment with it by sharing experiences with peers and conducting active experimentation in similar situations. Since sharing experiences is expected to develop our perspectives, it has been important in the education and practice of social workers.

Moreover, social work is considered both a science and an art form. It is a science because social workers are expected to use theoretical knowledge and apply scientific methods to solve problems. It is an art because they also use their skills to build relationships and communicate with people. Although the style of the act itself differs from person to person, sharing experiences in these areas is crucial for professional development. It helps social workers learn from others' experiences, gain new perspectives and develop new skills. Furthermore, it can help social workers reflect on their practices and identify areas for improvement.

Positive shared experiences can even help build confidence. They help us develop our professional practice and create a feeling of belongingness and connectedness among us, which is essential for the future of this profession. Moreover, they provide a sense of meaning to our practice and help us improve our skills working with people in similar situations. Sharing experiences will give us a bigger picture of the diversity of the country's social work practice.

Challenges of Sharing Experiences

Despite the positive outcomes of sharing experiences, there have been criticisms against this approach, especially regarding knowledge building. First, sharing personal experiences to build knowledge is not necessarily scientific. Individual experiences are often considered unreliable for assessing the effectiveness of an intervention since they are not based on solid evidence. In addition, knowledge is based on accumulating information through either experience or education. However, there are challenges in sharing experiences through education and training.

One of the challenges in presenting the experience is that the experiences of individual practitioners can be subjective and based primarily on their perceptions and emotions. In this case, although memories are stored, specific details are forgotten and replaced with new ones. It may be avoided if we look at our experiences from the third person and maintain objectivity, though.

However, some people argue that subjectivity is not wrong. In fact, our beliefs, emotions, values and norms represent our social reality. The behaviours of most people in this country are based on something other than scientific reasoning, but on their beliefs and traditional values.

Another challenge in sharing experiences is sometimes presented through storytelling, a method used in social work. However, when used for learning, it is important to clarify the actual experience verbally and in writing. In this regard, the lack of documentation has hurt the development of social work practice in the country.

Finally, sharing experiences in social work covers a vast field of practice, from working with individuals to creating social policy. This diversity of practice can make it somewhat difficult for everyone to reach a consensus during discussions.

Summary

The exchange of experiences is an essential part of social work practice. It can also help social workers develop new skills, gain new perspectives and reflect on their individual experiences. However, it is important to recognise the challenges associated with sharing experiences and work towards creating a supportive environment where social workers feel comfortable sharing their experiences.

Narratives from the Presentation [1]

Background

Several years ago, I first met Teru (Dr Higashida) when he came to our house to interview me about social work in Sri Lanka. During this interview, spoken in Sinhala, I learned that he had worked in Sri Lanka for quite some time. Then, when I was President of the Sri Lanka Association of Professional Social Workers (SLAPSW), we started dialogues on the development of social work in the country, based on our proposal and agreement. We also held several online discussions during the COVID-19 pandemic.

We have written a research paper based on a series of interviews and published it in an international journal (Higashida et al., 2022). In addition, we have discussed how to proceed with creating a joint conference. Then, after presenting this idea to the NISD (since the SLAPSW lacked suitable conference facilities), Mrs Shamini Attanayake accepted the proposal. As a result, this conference was organised. However, our work has only begun.

Conference Theme and Related Terms

We now focus on the conference theme: *Uncovering the Perspectives and Skills of Social Work Practices in the Sri Lankan Context*. In Sinhala, this is translated as *sri lamkika sandarbhaya tuḷa samaaja vaḍa paricaya, idiri darsanaya saha kusalataa anaavaranaya kirima* (ශ්‍රී ලාංකික සන්දර්භය තුළ සමාජ වැඩ පරිචය, ඉදිරි දර්ශනය සහ කුසලතා අනාවරණය කිරීම). Several Sinhala terms are used for these perspectives. For example, *paryaalookaya* (පර්යාලෝකය) is used in sociology. However, I use the word *idiri darśanaya* (ඉදිරි දර්ශනය) because *paryaalookaya* is extremely difficult. Meanwhile, in the Sri Lankan context, there are *sri lankaawee sandarbhaya tuḷa* (ශ්‍රී ලංකාවේ සන්දර්භය තුළ) and *samaaja wada paricaya* (සමාජ වැඩ පරිචය), which are roughly translated as 'uncovering the necessary skills' to identify the meaning of social work in Sri Lanka. In this conference, I will reveal the relevant issues, difficulty in defining social work in the Sri Lankan context, measures that we should take, advanced initiatives and significance and challenges of sharing social work experiences.

---

[1] Some of the contents overlap with those in the previous section, but they are still included because they contain important elements.

Significance of Exploring Social Work Experiences in Sri Lanka

Regarding my experience, I have taught social work, also called 'professional social work', for 31 years. Since the introduction of this field more than 71 years ago, there have been certain transformations in Sri Lanka. Let us begin by considering the relevance of this conference to the practice of social work in Sri Lanka. Now, this is called 'uncovering perspectives' and discussing the transformations in the country. Here, the word 'uncovering' is used, as perspectives on social work have not yet been openly discussed. Specifically, we tend to limit the discussion of social work to classrooms. Meanwhile, when students perform work in the field, they often find that social work is unknown to people, indicating that even after 71 years, social work remains a relatively unknown profession. This raises the following questions: Does the government or ministries understand social work? What is our place among working institutions? What is our legal position? Finally, what powers do we have?

One day, when I spoke to a social services officer in the Panadura Divisional Secretariat, he said, 'What you teach in social work science cannot be done here'. Furthermore, when I asked others who worked in the field, they said, 'Sir, it is a bit difficult to do these things in today's society'.

In light of the existing bureaucratic procedure, the following question is raised. Do we really understand the social work concept applicable in the Sri Lankan context? Since 1952, social work education has followed the scientific method and we have done social work in this way. It has been written that its development through industrialisation and modernisation is more applicable to Western culture than our society. While social work has been mainly developed in Western countries, with its individualistic societies, Sri Lanka is a community-based country. We have tried to take that and develop it here, but sometimes people do not necessarily accept social workers at their houses and talk about their problems. In fact, there are many similar situations and problems. This is the significant difference between Sri Lanka and the Western countries. Therefore, one of the objectives of this conference, namely, the exchange of knowledge and skills in social work practices in Sri Lanka, is vital for the future development of social work. This has been one of the major challenges that has prevented us from moving forward in the country.

Reconsidering Social Work and Its Concepts

It is also important to discuss the relevance of social work in Sri Lanka and the need for indigenous and local perspectives in this field. In this regard, I wrote a paper on the internationalisation of social work in Sri Lanka to discuss its historical and current features (Ranaweera, 2013). In general, many factors have affected such internationalisation. After presenting the findings, some people have asked 'Was there no social work before the introduction of social work in Sri Lanka in 1952?' and 'You have done it, but why do we not hear about this field?' Much work has been done, which might be recognised and called social work. They questioned whether these practices were not considered social work or only the practices of those who learned and studied it were considered social work.

Meanwhile, some models, such as the ABC model of indigenous social work, have been developed by scholars (Akimoto et al., 2020). Specifically, the ABC model distinguishes between the Westernisation of social work (the A-model), indigenous social work (the C-model) and a combination of the two aspects (the B-model). Furthermore, previous research has been conducted in Buddhist temples.

When I wrote about this, I realised there is still a problem defining social work in the Sri Lankan context. We know that the terms *samaaja seewaa* (සමාජ සේවා) or *samaaja wada* (සමාජ වැඩ) have been used in social services in Sri Lankan higher education since the beginning. Currently, university degrees use the terms *samaaja krtya* (සමාජ කෘත්‍ය) or *samaaja kaaryayan* (සමාජ කාර්යයන්). Our association is presented in the parliamentary act of the Sri Lanka Association of Professional Social Workers (SLAPSW) in English. In Sinhala, it is called *samaaja karya vrttiyavedinge samgamaya* (සමාජ කාර්ය වෘත්තියවේදීන්ගේ සංගමය). In this case, *samaaja kaaryaya* (සමාජ කාර්යය) means 'social work'. Regarding the degrees, it is called 'social professionalism' or *samaaja vrttiyavedi upaadhiya* (සමාජ වෘත්තියවේදී උපාධිය), meaning 'Degree in Social Work'.

These findings suggest that society has yet to find a relevant word in Sinhala or a definition for this field. Hence, related organisations, institutions and the government must be aware of this issue. If we consider our long history, even rulers, kings and royalty have engaged in some form of social services. Moreover, various structures were built, such as resting places and alms halls. More recently, when the 2004 Indian Ocean earthquake and tsunami occurred, neighbours and relatives were the first to arrive and provide help. Thus, can such actions be considered as social work?

The International Meaning of Social Work and Its Application in Sri Lanka

Sometimes, social work is referred to as 'charity work', although this is not necessarily true. To better understand the meaning of social work and differentiate it from charity work, we must discuss and understand what it is. When we take social work via services, we must discuss its history. The Commission on Social Services was established under the British Empire during colonial times. The Jennings Report describes the most popular social services and network. According to the recommendations of the report, the social services department was established. According to the Jennings Report, regardless of the number of shortcomings in society, people are firmly bound to help one another. Thus, there was no need for government intervention. Over time, the government intervened, creating additional problems by introducing the poor laws of England. Then we talk about it under welfare services.

A recent study by UNICEF stated that there were many social services workers in Sri Lanka. This raises the question of whether their practices are considered social work. According to the Global Definition of the Social Work Profession, social work is a practice-based profession and academic discipline that promotes social change and development, social cohesion and the empowerment and liberation of people (IFSW & IASSW, 2014). Based on this definition, does social work in Sri Lanka meet such criteria? Is it a recognised profession in Sri Lanka? Clearly, it has not been officially accepted.

Recently, there was a discussion on the radio with a representative from the UGC. He talked about universities and universities with degree holding in Sri Lanka, but did not mention NISD. This indicates that social work has not yet been officially recognised as a profession and not as an academic discipline or standard of practice in Sri Lanka. Therefore, paradoxically, there is no social work practice in Sri Lanka, as we define words based on international definitions. Also, there is no monitoring of social workers since a code of ethics and related regulations have yet to be implemented.

What Should We Do?

Sometimes, examining our history can be beneficial in determining how we can achieve this in Sri Lanka. Previously, when I was teaching a diploma course, the curriculum included a history of social work in Sri Lanka. I recall briefly discussing this when developing the curriculum. Although this subject no longer exists, we must continue to investigate the values, beliefs and norms of people in society, especially when helping those in need.

Moreover, we must continue to consider the meaning of social work in light of the beliefs, values and attitudes of people towards knowledge creation in Sri Lanka. If we can build a dialogue based on these issues, it would greatly help to recognise social work in the country.

When I gave a group presentation with researchers from the Asia-Pacific region, I was asked about the definition of social work in Sri Lanka. I quickly stated that we still do not have a proper definition in Sri Lanka. Even the President of the Asian and Pacific Association for Social Work Education (APASWE) stated that the dialogue is ongoing in most countries. Hence, one cannot apply the Western definition of social work to a specific culture. Therefore, continuing discussions with social work practitioners in the Sri Lankan context is the best step to take.

Significance of Sharing Social Work Experiences

Dr Higashida requested that I primarily discuss the significance of sharing social work practice. At this point, we can safely state that social work is about helping people. However, knowledge of this field does not automatically result in the implementation of social work.

For example, we teach students and they take notes, complete the assignments and pass the examinations. Subsequently, their knowledge is often replaced by practical experience after entering the field. This is one of the main reasons why we have added fieldwork in the course of study. If they only knew, it would be difficult for them to carry out social work practice. They must practice social work while learning from the field. We develop our knowledge through practice. Otherwise, such accumulation of knowledge from books and theories will not necessarily translate into actions. Sharing experiences is essential for learning. Therefore, after the field work has been completed, we usually hold seminars to exchange these experiences as a way of learning.

According to the experiential learning theory (Kolb et al., 2014), we obtain concrete experiences from working. As for social workers, they develop new knowledge through abstract conceptualisations; subsequently, they discuss what has worked, create action plans and experiment in a new situation.

Benefits of Sharing Practical Experiences

When we share positive experiences and feedback, we build self-confidence. Through discussing it, we internalise it. It is a necessary thing for developing the competencies of social workers. In addition, we can also develop our feelings and connections with others by sharing such experiences.

Therefore, I previously asked a class whether they had ever maintained a diary and discussed the entries with others. Subsequently, I asked if they would be willing to share their entries in a public presentation. Therefore, it would build the presenter's confidence and provide us with a larger picture of the development of social work in the country.

Challenges of Sharing Practical Experiences

Despite the benefits of sharing experiences, some challenges remain. First, some people need to scientifically consider personal experiences, even though it is a Western type of thinking. When we say something, we refer to some experience: what we did in the past. There is a level of memory loss after which specific details are replaced by new (or fictional) ones based on personal values and feelings. We may call this subjective thinking. However, if subjective feelings are eliminated and we become more objective, we can use these experiences for personal development in social work. This is the value of sharing practice experiences.

In particular, students tend to present their experiences as stories when sharing such experiences. During such instances, I suggest reflecting on what has been done and determining what can be improved. In certain instances, they say that everything is good. However, how many of these future social workers have written and published their findings? After months of fieldwork, these experiences could be the basis for a thesis. At this point, the following question is raised: To what extent are we using our experiences to understand what is happening in Sri Lanka? In other words, are social work students only performing fieldwork to receive a diploma or degree or are they striving to improve the field of social work? That means that Western type of rational thinking is something we do not have. We have to accept it.

In addition, various religions in Sri Lanka should be considered. Accordingly, acknowledging religious beliefs, values and norms in social work practice is crucial regardless of how much we mention scientific methods or Western thinking. This is another challenge in sharing practical experience in the Sri Lankan context.

Conclusion

In conclusion, social work includes various benefits and challenges, especially in the Sri Lankan context. Therefore, effective understanding of the meaning of social work and what it entails is imperative. Furthermore, since sharing experiences has been shown to be extremely effective, we should continue to take advantage of this approach and use it to transform social work into a major profession in the country. We can start by focusing on the results of these presentations at this conference.

Chapter 2: Volunteerism and Social Work

M.T.R. Shamini Attanayake

National Institute of Social Development

Abstract: Volunteerism is providing time and skills for the benefit of others, rather than for financial gain. Furthermore, in an employment-related context, it concerns the methods and tools employers use to support volunteers. Additionally, it enables people to help and serve others altruistically. When people take the initiative to help people in the community and support philanthropic causes, they also improve the community by creating stronger bonds and forming lasting relationships. Therefore, non-profit organisations can use groups of dedicated volunteers to achieve goals and make the world safer.

Social workers are trained practitioners who work with all types of vulnerable people, groups and communities to help them learn to live better lives. In this case, those in need may suffer from poverty, discrimination or other social injustices. In particular, social workers and volunteers are engaged in the same type of work; however, the difference is in their training and methods in general.

Volunteerism has a long history in Sri Lanka, creating a good balance between social services and volunteering. Here, instead of traditional volunteer services, skills-based social work is performed through practical skills, while social services are performed with a charitable objective. Policy management methods can be used for volunteers employed by organisations during formal training. Here, the integrative approach to social work is important. Many voluntary organisations in Sri Lanka can be classified into the public and non-governmental sectors. There are rural development societies and community-based rehabilitation programmes in the public sector. For the latter, they include the Red Cross Society and the Sarvodaya Sramadhana Association. Meanwhile, there are many religious-based organisations in the country. Thus, it is important to share the knowledge and skills of social workers with volunteers in order for the latter to engage in welfare work in a more formal, systematic and well-trained manner.

Keywords: Volunteerism, Social work, Social services, Integrated social work

Traditional Community and Volunteerism

Sri Lanka has a long history of volunteerism and is very familiar to our community. This introduction will briefly explain why we discuss volunteerism and social work. Volunteering has generally been considered the 'donation of labour', commonly known as *shramadaana*. In this sense, all communities work together to achieve a common goal. This raises the following questions: What does volunteerism mean? What are the differences between volunteerism and social work?

Generally, Sri Lanka is a traditional community in which individual volunteerism has contributed over the centuries. Meanwhile, free of labour charges, organised volunteerism has taken some time to earn a dominant place in society. However, it has become a major factor in the country's economic and social development.

Sri Lanka also has a long history of people working together for agricultural purposes. For example, in agriculture and agriculture, everyone works together and without labour charges. As a social responsibility, this volunteerism supports or changes the lives of those in the community and creates long-lasting bonds.

Most definitions of volunteerism generally include three key elements: having free will, gaining no financial reward and helping beneficiaries. Moreover, volunteerism is essential because it enables people to help others. When individuals participate in such activities, they can improve the community and build long-lasting bonds. However, why do people engage in volunteerism? Motivational functions for voluntarism include values in our community, norms, practice, understanding, social care and proactive ones: Cultural values are very important in the Sri Lankan context. In other words, people are likely to have multiple motivations based on their personal and cultural values while promoting community development.

We know that volunteers in Western countries, such as United Nations (UN) volunteers, are sometimes partially paid. On the contrary, volunteers in our country contribute to community development, but are not paid in general. Volunteering has numerous benefits, such as gaining a sense of purpose and community, meeting new friends, improving social skills and self-esteem, gaining valuable practical skills and having fun. Furthermore, we can understand the attitudes of others and change ours accordingly. In other words, the benefits are extensive.

Differences between Volunteerism and Social Work

Why do we call it 'social work'? We know that the Global Definition of the Social Work Profession includes helping vulnerable people improve their lives and well-being and empowering them. This is a straightforward definition of social work. Then what is the difference between volunteerism and social work? Social workers receive professional training and education and are expected to have scientific knowledge on methods they can apply to solve people's problems practically. Social work can be especially helpful for vulnerable people, groups and communities suffering from poverty, discrimination or social injustice, while social workers and volunteer workers commit the same work. In other words, social workers work with vulnerable people, groups and communities, while volunteers also work with them. The primary difference is in the training and methods they use. Social workers are expected to be highly trained, whereas volunteers are not. Another difference is the type of welfare and social services that they perform: social workers would do this in their development manner using scientific methods. However, both parties have a common goal: Help vulnerable people in the community improve their daily lives and well-being.

Relationship in the Sri Lankan Context

As stated above, there is a good balance between social work and volunteerism in Sri Lanka, both related to traditional societal functions. Although there are many related terms, such as social services, social welfare or social development, they do not necessarily have the same meaning as social work. For example, social services, voluntary services and social welfare provide support under social welfare programmes such as donations and welfare activities provided by the government. In this sense, *Samrudhi* is a government social welfare programme that provides schoolchildren, for example, with clothes and books. These are some welfare services provided by the government sector. Meanwhile, social development, another related term, involves developing policies and implementing related programmes with planned engagement.

Considering these terms, what is social work practice? This is a significant topic today. It involves the professional application of social work based on its values, principles and techniques. Moreover, it focuses on connecting relevant services to vulnerable individuals, families and groups in their respective communities. In social work, we also have a theory on how to work with people. Unlike volunteers, social workers attempt to understand people's problems from a scientific perspective. In this regard, what types of theory do we use when working with people?

What are the components of social work practice? Western-rooted social work theory includes social case, group and community work. In this regard, social workers not only work with people, but also attempt to understand each person and assess his/her needs and environmental conditions to create an effective intervention. Then they initiate an organised process at three levels of social work: macro, meso and micro. Specifically, the microlevel focuses on individuals and family units, including their relationships, while the meso level focuses on the surrounding community. At the macro level, it focuses on system-wide issues and relevant policy formulation.

From the basic perspective of Western-rooted professional social work, there are five stages of practices, namely, engagement, assessment planning, intervention, evaluation and termination. Meanwhile, what are the main domains of practice in social work? They include professionalism, values and ethics, diversity, rights, justice, economic well-being, knowledge, clinical reflection and analysis, intervention and skills.

Although social workers respect the diversity of values and ethics, knowledge and methods are also necessary. As mentioned by Mr Ranaweera (Chapter 1), more efforts are required to develop culturally relevant social work in the Sri Lankan context. Specifically, we must 'open our eyes' to the situation and consider why we have not yet explored indigenous social work in the country. The indigenous practice and knowledge must be developed to work with communities. We may use theories rooted in Western countries, but we must consider the Sri Lankan context and develop indigenous social work.

Perhaps we can learn from the philosophy of Buddhist social work. Lord Buddha was the first social worker (Wickramasinghe, 2020). We can also explore indigenous social work and promote practices in the Sri Lankan context to develop such communities and solve their respective problems.

Meanwhile, social services with charitable objectives will likely differ from those of social workers. The policy management methods for volunteer services and reporting of volunteers can be carried out under formal training. Social workers with systematic training are expected to be change agents for our communities.

Conclusion

At this point, we have clarified the differences between social work and volunteerism. Regarding social work, it is based on scientific knowledge and related policies. However, we must practice in our community and develop social work at the indigenous level. We must explore indigenous social work methods and views and apply them at the grassroots level because we now rely on Western-rooted theories and techniques. In this regard, the SLAPSW focuses on developing indigenous social work in Sri Lanka.

Meanwhile, we also plan to introduce a programme involving three organisations, that is, UNICEF, NISD and SLAPSW, to further develop the field of social work in Sri Lanka. Although we are fortunate to have the support of UNICEF, we require professional social workers who understand the differences between social work, social services and social development in the Sri Lankan context. These individuals are pioneers in this critical endeavour. In summary, it is our duty and responsibility. We must 'open our eyes' and focus on how we can develop social work in Sri Lanka in an indigenous way.

Conclusion

PART II:

PRACTICAL EXPERIENCES

Chapter 3: Social Work Experiences in Community-Based Rehabilitation

Saroja P. Weththewa
Chief Social Services Officer, Anuradhapura

Editors' note: This chapter was added to this book because it contributes significantly to the overall theme. The following narratives are from an interview between Ms Weththewa (a social services officer) and Dr Masateru Higashida on 1 November 2023. Ms Weththewa, often called '*Saroja Miss*' in Anuradhapura, has conducted grassroots activities with people with disabilities, including community-based rehabilitation (CBR), for over 30 years. Furthermore, Dr Higashida has worked with her as an overseas volunteer social worker, dispatched by the Japan International Cooperation Agency (JICA) and conducted related activities with people with disabilities in Anuradhapura from January 2013 to January 2015 (Higashida, 2015).

> *Keywords:* Grassroots practices, Socio-culturally relevant practices, Disability-inclusive development, Passion

Work History

Saroja: As for my work history, I started in this position on 1 February 1994, first in the Thambuththegama Divisional Secretariat and then in the Galnewa Divisional Secretariat. Subsequently, I returned to Rajanganaya and then to Thambuththegama in November 2021.

Higashida: Did you have an opportunity to learn about social work?

Saroja: I had two weeks of CBR training. Subsequently, I worked with JICA volunteers and learned from their experiences. I also worked with JICA volunteers in Galnewa from 2003 to 2008.

Higashida: How did you go into the field and meet people?

Saroja: Since meeting people with disabilities at the Divisional Secretariat office proved to be not enough and ineffective, my only choice was to visit their places of residence, observe their home environment and their family background. In this way, I was able to understand and assess their needs and provide them with the necessary support and services.

This means that after I started the practical engagement, I could meet and work with most of our disabled people in the area. In this case, disability is not something unfamiliar. We may also be disabled depending on the environment. Moreover, our own children could be disabled. Our relatives may be disabled. Regarding my attitude, I simply treated each person as if they were my own child or family member. I reflected on their living difficulties related to mental or physical conditions and approaches to help them deal with these issues. This truly inspired me to help them. This is how it happened.

Practice Experiences

Higashida: Then, you started to do various activities, including group activities related to culture and religion, as well as community work. Why did you think of doing such things?

Saroja: Currently, it is a little less, but when we came to the service, people with disabilities were a somewhat marginalised part of society. Their social participation was likely limited. However, they want to enjoy the same privileges as ordinary people. For example, some of our people with disabilities are too old to go to vocational training centres in our Department of Social Services, while those treating diseases need help with their own work. Since the recruitment of additional people in our vocational training centre was limited, I came up with the idea of developing the skills and knowledge of children with disabilities in the village so that they could eventually become self-employed or at least find ways to live independently, without depending on their parents and siblings.

Simultaneously, some JICA volunteers and I got together and visited our vocational training centres, after which we considered the available courses and relevant resources. Specifically, we explore what courses could be offered in our village. Likewise, our 'classes' (*pantiya* or mobile workshops) were focused on providing occupational and social skills to children with disabilities in our village. Now, some people are self-employed and support their families.

Regarding religion, many people here are Buddhists. In this regard, Buddhist philosophy indicates that a person is born with disabilities due to bad actions or evil deeds committed by them in their previous life, as a negative karma (Liyanage, 2017). When it comes to people with disabilities, they have a lower chance of doing 'good deeds' in society. Even if there is charitable or charitable work, they do not have the opportunity to offer requisites or perform religious activities. To allow people with disabilities to participate in such religious activities, we conducted a monthly *Sil Samadam* programme in each village (Higashida, 2016).

Through this programme, people in these villages learned that those with disabilities could do such things. The disabled people of that village gave alms. Also, they offered requirements to Buddhist monks through our programmes. They became interested in participating in religious activities. Subsequently, the participation in religious activities became a regular occurrence for them, which greatly helped them.

Furthermore, we helped them make things that they could sell and trade at fairs to earn money. This indicates that working together with society to improve the lives of the disadvantaged is possible. It also suggests that people with disabilities need to be developed in all aspects, similar to people without disabilities.

Roots of her Practices

Higashida: How did you develop this idea before joining social services?

Saroja: As I mentioned above, I believe that people with disabilities should receive the same treatment as those without disabilities. Regarding my background, I first met people with disabilities when I was a child. At that time, I helped people with financial difficulties by giving them books and pens and teaching them about certain topics. I enjoyed doing such things and it made me think about how their situations can be improved. Eventually, I got my current job as a social services officer, where I continue to help those in need.

Higashida: As a senior practitioner, what idea would you give young social services workers?

Saroja: There are three things that young social services workers should keep in mind. First, it is important to implement a disability-inclusive programme, such as the CBR programme and take our duties and responsibilities out of the office. Second, we need to look out for people with disabilities in each division and truly understand their life situations as well as mental and physical conditions. In this sense, we must be there as someone other than an officer. We must be compassionate and caring with the sole purpose of improving their lives and well-being. Third, we must establish a level of trust in which they can openly share their problems and needs. We need to get close to the person, like their good friends, so that they can openly share their ideas, wishes as well as problems faced, sometimes even misconceptions, without fear. Then, if we get close to them with a trustable relationship, then we can provide relevant and available information.

Sometimes people (e.g. parents) just expect financial welfare support from the government, which is unlikely to be used to improve the living conditions of disabled people. Instead of just distributing welfare allowances, if we can get close to them, we can enhance their capability directly, including any relevant programmes for their future life and employment. In this way, they will not only contribute to the country's economy, but will also be able to live independently in society. This is what we should think about as social services officers. Again, I believe that our fundamental duty is beyond giving them welfare benefits.

Difficult Conditions

Higashida: Are there officers in the CBR who perform activities like you?

Saroja: Yes, there are. Every division includes an officer who performs social services. However, the practice conditions are not good due to the challenging economic situation in the country. Sometimes people with disabilities must commute to our programmes with another person or relative, although the cost of transportation is high, causing great inconvenience. However, in most cases, the right person always comes along.

Regarding manufacturing products in classes (mobile workshops), there is a problem obtaining raw materials, especially in rural areas such as Anuradhapura. Sometimes, the demand for handicrafts decreases, unless one sells essential products for the home. For example, customers are likelier to purchase a broom, instead of a beautiful rug or vase. In this economic situation, selling decorative items, such as necklaces, pendants, greeting cards, brooches and wall decorations, has become more difficult in this area.

Ideas for Grassroots Practices and Their Impact

Saroja: I first facilitated the gathering of children with disabilities. Specifically, we started the classes with the idea of developing each child's capabilities rather than creating and selling products. First, we collected the papers discarded in the offices and put them on the covers. Then, it took about three or four months for our disabled people to learn how to apply glue to those covers. These covers were made to develop skills rather than generate income.

As the children's capabilities and skills gradually developed, we also improved their qualities. Additionally, we discussed different ways to create products for the economy, based on the support and knowledge of stakeholders, such as officials in different sectors. In fact, our work with people with disabilities was officially recognised as a good-practice case, after which it was implemented in all divisions. Because we realised that they have the capabilities, we initiated them to developing relevant activities.

Higashida: Finally, has the status of people with disabilities changed in Rajanganaya?

Saroja: Yes, there have been some changes. Those who were once isolated at home have found friends and support. They also enthusiastically attend classes and religious activities like their normal counterparts.

Wishes and Thoughts

Saroja: I would like to say that it would be good for our country and our economy if people with disabilities had professional skills, reasonable accommodations and access to facilities. Thus, they can live in society, similar to people without disabilities, without being marginalised. In such real inclusive environments, doing something special for them is likely to be unnecessary. I think it is necessary to provide them with the reasonable accommodation and necessary facilities to promote their ordinary living and contribute to society as a citizen.

Higashida: Regarding Western-rooted concepts, some types of care are suitable, but others are not. What do you think?

Saroja: Currently, technology in Western countries is highly advanced. For example, people with disabilities can use public transportation, as some buses can accommodate wheelchairs. However, such people are unable to do this in Sri Lanka. For example, a person in a wheelchair cannot get on a bus without being personally lifted onto the vehicle. The same situation occurs in rail transportation. However, it is easy to observe that someone nearby naturally helps them to help each other. In other words, such technological capabilities are required for all. Although there is a law that all public buildings in Sri Lanka must have accessible facilities, it is yet to be fully implemented in all buildings. This remains a problem in our society.

Stakeholders

Saroja: Officers in other sections, such as youth services officers, should be able to speak openly about young people with disabilities and support them through various activities such as camps and training courses. When youth services officers worked with young people in events and programmes, disabled young people were included in our division. Not only social services officers, but also other officers/actors should have an opportunity to support the development of this population. Another example is that sports officers should have an opportunity to improve the sports skills of people with disabilities. In other words, officers in all fields should not exclude people with disabilities and should simply treat them as ordinary citizens. Only if we come together can we progress in the social situations of people with disabilities.

Regarding Social Services Officers

Saroja: The other social services officers also perform their duties and receive CBR training. Since they came to work, CBR has been the central part of their work.

Our progress review meeting is held monthly at the District Secretariat in Anuradhapura. Through these meetings, social services officers can gain and exchange knowledge. In addition, the Department of Social Services offers a training programme in which they can share relevant practical knowledge. Currently, a sociology or related degree is considered appropriate for social services officers. However, numerous officers do not have the relevant degrees.

New officers often gain experience by working under a supervisory senior officer when they join the workforce. I have noticed that when new officers are appointed, they enter the field without an adequate understanding of the actual practices. However, they must do it because of their duties. Some perform their duties and strive to improve; others dislike the work and eventually leave. However, I can safely say that not all officers do this and that these attitudes vary from person to person.

Future

Higashida: How many more years will you work?

Saroja: Exactly 1 year. After that, I will retire and personally help people with disabilities. Yes, in this case, it will be without pay. However, my objective will be to simply provide my labour and to further develop my knowledge when the opportunity arises.

44

Photo 1 *Activities in the field in 2013/2014*

Left: A mobile workshop with people with disabilities
Right: Community assessment with CBR volunteers

Chapter 4: Experiences of a *Grama Niladhari* from a Social Work Perspective

E.A. Upeksha Piyumanthi
Grama Niladhari

Abstract: Generally, social workers in Sri Lanka are not based on professional ethics, although they offer services under various titles. Due to various political and capitalist class pressures, all officials must provide some type of service. Therefore, there is a lack of service flow to marginalised populations. Furthermore, there are limited opportunities for marginalised population groups to work, sometimes violating their rights or human dignity. In particular, social welfare programmes implemented in the past have increased dependency mentality among many individuals while keeping economic development at a minimum. The main reason for this is that components of programmes, such as the development approach, free healthcare, education and poverty alleviation, have caused people to become more dependent.

For many rural people in Sri Lanka, they believe that the government should meet the basic needs of all people and that it should be responsible for all social issues. Despite decades of universal welfare, it is rare to find that a community has been empowered. However, it is crucial to identify the strengths of rural communities and empower them through interventions so that religious and cultural elements and traditional customs are protected. As a first step, this must begin at the family level, with the guidance of trained social workers with relevant knowledge and experience to serve as an effective mediator.

In this chapter, I will share my practical experiences in the *Grama Niladhari* division, especially with regard to the economic crisis in Sri Lanka. In addition, I will discuss how I empowered my community during this crisis.

Keywords: Marginalised population groups, Social empowerment, Rural communities

Personal Background

Regarding my background, I am a *Grama Niladhari* (civil servant working at the village level) in Kandy, located in the Kundasalaya Divisional Secretariat. I accepted this position in 2009 and have worked as an official in grassroots public administration for the past 14 years. During my childhood, I became interested in social services, volunteering and leadership. This was the main reason why I became a Grama Niladhari. Later, I received the short-term and long-term training programmes required for my duties. I also earned an Advanced Diploma in Social Work in 2018 and am currently studying for an MSW.

Social Contexts in a *Grama Niladhari* Division

A *Grama Niladhari* is an officer who runs the administrative mechanism at the grassroots level, dealing with various services offered to a person from birth to death. They also serve as facilitators, service providers and legal advocates who implement government policies at the village level.

The 692 Kundasalaya South *Grama Niladhari* Division is where I am assigned. This division, which comprises 22 villages, includes one of the highest population densities in the Kandy district. Specifically, this division includes 2,252 households and a population density of more than 9,000 persons per sq. km. As shown in Figure 1, this division includes various ethnicities, religions and social statuses. As for income distribution, the villages include upper, middle and lower classes.

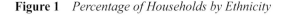

Figure 1 *Percentage of Households by Ethnicity*

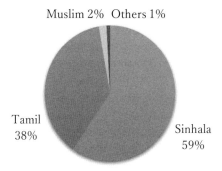

Identified Issues

Based on my service in this division, I can classify the issues in the villages into three parts: economic, social and environmental. As for the economic problems are mainly at the lower economic level, with weaknesses in income, expenditure control and financial management. In addition, there is a high level of poverty and dependency, with some instances in which the elderly are isolated. In this case, the elderly are left alone at home due to the recent social changes in our country. This was widely observed in our division. Other problems in this division include the noticeable loss of mental happiness, cultural and religious problems and environmental issues. For the latter, there was an instance in which three houses were spread over a relatively small plot of land. Due to such population density, I had to ensure that each household maintained an effective waste management and disposal system. Otherwise, the risk of infectious diseases, such as dengue, would have increased. In fact, several cases of dengue have been reported during my tenure. In general, my interventions have been crucial to this division. After identifying all these issues, my intervention was presented to the division.

Experience in Social Work Practice

In light of the economic crisis, my work focused on the welfare of individuals. For example, I proposed that some people spend part of their funds and provide seeds and planting materials to others at a minimum cost (instead of free). A dependency mentality should not be developed in a social worker. When we get something for free, we tend to lose a sense of empowerment and focus. Therefore, through my proposal, people became interested in planting because they could only obtain seeds and planting materials after spending their own money.

A garbage problem also became an environmental issue in the division. Therefore, considering the community's economic development, I selected vacant lands at the village level and worked to produce compost and organic fertilisers. I am delighted to report that some villagers produced organic fertilisers for their own community and produced enough for sale. As for the latter, they earned a significant amount of money.

In addition, I collected information about three villages and built an exchange centre. In the past, we had an exchange economy system that was united through our culture and religion. I reintroduced this system, after which the people used it to share their excess fruits and vegetables from their gardens and their clothes and other usable school equipment with others. In this case, if one child's shoes cannot be used and are of good quality, then the family can bring them to the centre, after which another child can take them. This exchange system has been successful and continues today.

Meanwhile, small-scale industrialists received self-employment training to establish their respective businesses. For example, a 100-m reserve is generally covered with vegetation at the Mahaweli River border. During the rainy season, it becomes an extremely fertile area. Therefore, I discussed this with the Mahaweli Development Authority and distributed parts of the reserve to young people interested in cultivating the land. After their successful work, they sold their bounty of fruits and vegetables.

Finally, in my division, many people practice animal farming and agriculture. However, one of the main problems was the loose cattle, which started to damage crops. Then, as a *Grama Niladhari* official, I had to use my powers as a Justice of the Peace. In this regard, the owners of these animals were punished and compensation was collected. Ultimately, the owners made the necessary interventions by keeping them in the stables rather than freeing them. I am ready to deal with such challenging issues when faced with them.

Perspective of Social Work in Sri Lanka

At this point, let me briefly describe my perspective on social work in Sri Lanka. In the narrow sense, there are almost no professions called 'social workers' in Sri Lanka. Social work is generally performed under other titles and positions. However, the problem is that ethics and values are not being implemented. Meanwhile, various universal welfare programmes are being conducted in Sri Lanka. Due to these programmes, the dependency of individuals has increased, whereas economic development has decreased. Therefore, our country, which used to be a developing country, has become a country with a poor economy.

Discussion with the Floor

Piyumanthi: I recognise that humans have a substantial amount of power. However, the majority have become completely dependent on welfare campaigns such as those in *Samurdhi*. They tend to believe that the government should provide them with everything they need. In fact, they often come to us and say 'we want a house, a job, a bag of stuff'. I agree that the government should help society to a certain level; however, it should help people develop themselves by building their capacity to earn

Photo 2   *Activities in the Division*

an income. This tendency is especially prevalent in the lower income social class, and it should be changed.

Participant: I agree that there is a dependency mentality in villages. What method did you follow as a social worker to eliminate such dependency? How did you launch your work on these issues such as the creation of compost fertiliser cultivation and the intervention in the animal problem? How successful was it?

Piyumanthi: I will answer your questions by mentioning the fact that my division includes many widows with children. An outsider might think that these people cannot work and that no one cares for the children. Hence, I created a successful women's society called '*Pragathi*' in which I gathered these widows and provided them with opportunities for self-employment. Among this group, some were able to use their sewing skills to create excellent decorative products.

I want to talk about one of those women. When her husband died fighting in the Galle area, she was a mother of two with another child on the way. However, we trained her in soapmaking and she currently produces and sells soap to businesses and earns a good income. Therefore, I recognised the capabilities of the woman.

Another example is of a Tamil woman with a husband with disabilities. Previously, he worked for an aluminium company in a different district. However, he lost his job because of his disabilities. Subsequently, after receiving the right training, we connected him with a private bank to obtain loans at subsidised interest rates. Today, he runs a small factory and produces aluminium-related products at home. In this regard, I empowered the family using the husband's capabilities.

Chapter 5: Empowering Parents Towards the Future Security of Children with Disabilities

K.H. Chamara Kumarasinghe
Social Services Officer

Abstract: Generally, childbirth is a special occasion for parents. A mother physically devotes around nine months in general, receives close attention from her relatives and expects her child to have a lifetime of happiness. However, a child with physical or mental disabilities is not the expectation of parents. In a culturally diverse country, such as Sri Lanka, individuals' roles in society are diverse. However, people with special needs are viewed from a narrow perspective; the social opinion is that children with disabilities and special needs should receive sympathy or pity, since they place significant burdens on the family. Therefore, the arrival of a child with a disability is a significant challenge for a mother and a father. As a pregnant woman receiving special attention, having a child with special needs can change her lifestyle and the lives of her husband and relatives. In fact, members of such families fear the reaction of society.

The government of Sri Lanka pays special attention to the nutrition of pregnant women, childbirth and children up to the age of five, as a social welfare measure. Meanwhile, local health departments, medical centres and family health officers regularly monitor children on an equal basis. In other words, they are not classified as healthy or disabled children with special needs. However, health departments and social workers should also pay special attention to parents of children with disabilities, especially their mental health conditions. Specifically, they should provide guidance on how to properly develop a child with special needs, without being an additional burden to the family and society. In this case, social services officers and social workers can be vital in mentally and economically empowering parents. In the absence of proper guidance, the lives of parents of children with disabilities will most likely be difficult, especially in a culturally bound country such as Sri Lanka. Thus, it is important to strengthen their capabilities for the future welfare of

52

these children.

Keywords: Childbirth, Social services, Cultural matters, Public sector

Background

Regarding my background, I currently work as a social services officer in the Katana Divisional Secretariat while studying for an MSW at the NISD. My main topic of interest is determining how to strengthen parents, both mentally and economically, for the future security of their children with physical and mental disabilities. Regarding parents of normal children under five years of age, parents have been seen carrying newborn babies on the street numerous times. However, seeing parents with a child with a disability on the street is rare.

Selected Area

At this point, I would like to focus on a field study programme conducted in the Katana Divisional Secretariat. The Divisional Secretariat included two divisions of the Medical Officer of Health (MOH), namely, Katana and Seeduwa. Another was related to the Board of Investment in the Free Trade Zone. Consequently, I chose the Seeduwa Division because I believed it was the best place to acquire information regarding children at the state level. After obtaining official permission from the authorities, I obtained information from the family health officers and *Grama Niladhari* officers, the primary officials at the village level. In other words, as a social services officer, I worked as a team with the officers of these other sections.

Challenges

However, in this case, the information received was different. For example, family health officers missed some information, while some *Grama Niladhari* officers did not know if these families had such children. Then I recognised some areas where I found 22 children, 12 girls and 10 boys. As a percentage of children born at that time, it was 4%. As a matter of duty, I started to conduct my fieldwork. I observed the unexpected challenges faced by parents with children with disabilities. Birth itself is an unpredictable phenomenon, but having their child's impairments was likely to be challenges equally spread between mother and father. This was also in addition to the challenges of interacting with relatives and others in society.

Cultural Matters

Next, we will touch on cultural issues that are directly associated with the theme of this conference. During my fieldwork, when I visited several houses, some simply said 'No, we do not have such a child'. Such responses were often given by the grandparents but not by the parents. This indicates that the grandparents were hiding them or embarrassed about them. In such cases, it was difficult for me to be directly involved, even in a professional manner. However, I had to be involved in family matters after prior notice was given to them through a family health officer and a *Grama Niladhari* officer.

We are always confined culturally. To date, Sri Lankan families still consider the birth of a child with disabilities an ominous and shameful aspect. The main issue is the uncertainty of the future, which parents and their extended families share. This is also due to the cultural and religious ideologies of the country and the family history. Sometimes, even in certain cases, society shows that seeing children with disabilities is ominous. Therefore, in this case, instead of giving me a positive response, the grandparents thought of their grandchild in a negative light.

Government Initiatives

At this point, the following question is raised: Where does our government stand? As stated previously, the government is heavily involved during pregnancy: essential services are provided through family health officers, with the expectation that a healthy baby will be born. Thus, infant mortality and malnutrition rates are relatively low. However, there is a missing piece of the puzzle. Although a child with a disability is born, treating, administering medications and measuring weight, among others, are all performed by midwives basically in the same manner without adequate, relevant support.

Current health systems have pros and cons for children with disabilities and their parents. In my opinion, government intervention is too insufficient to address the mentality of parents of children with disabilities. Although every Divisional Secretariat includes counsellors, such parents are reluctant to share their situations and address their needs. Therefore, proper support and guidance should be provided to address the mental conditions of these parents primarily.

Parental Mental Strength

It is a challenge for parents from the moment a baby is born. Thus, interventions must be strengthened to address parental mental conditions. Because I am an interprofessional, not a professional, with a governmental position, it is debatable whether it is appropriate to consider my practice with what is commonly referred to as social work. However, based on my fieldwork, this aspect must be addressed from a social work perspective by highlighting the strengths of both parents and the child, rather than simply focusing on cultural confinements and difficulties. In other words, having a disability does not necessarily mean that a child can do nothing in their life. In fact, with proper training and education, they can develop their capabilities under reasonable accommodations.

Social Workers and Social Services Officers

As a social services officer, if social workers are available, they could supervise and guide parents of children with disabilities, such as focusing on the issues related to taking care of the children and removing social challenges. Furthermore, they could implement comprehensive and relevant practices, blending social services with social work, which empower parents with the strength to accept their children's disabilities. Social services officers, family health officers, counsellors and other stakeholders can comprehensively offer such psycho-social support. Social services officers should primarily address this, since they have fewer barriers to providing such support. In this case, this support includes improving their financial condition, as children with disabilities tend to require medicine, which can have a financial impact on the household.

Finally, the parents' education is compulsory. Specifically, parents should be aware of the nature of their child's disabilities and rethink the saying 'To whom is this future for?' Therefore, if parents are motivated and fully grounded, it will be much easier to develop the child's future capabilities, regardless of the socio-cultural background.

Discussion with the Floor

Participant: Based on your experience and knowledge, are there any proposals from your end that can help overcome this issue? As a social services worker knowledgeable on both ends, in this type of forum that discusses these practices, are there suggestions based on your experience and knowledge?

Kumarasinghe: First, a thorough study should be conducted on individual families. From my experience, I noticed that mothers take responsibility approximately 90% of the time. For example, I heard one mother say: 'I am the reason for the birth of this child'. In another instance, two mothers surprisingly said that their husbands believed that they needed to die. In this case, these mothers had no one to speak to about this issue. However, after maintaining connections with them four times, they opened their minds and felt a sense of peace. In general, such issues, which sometimes differ between mothers and fathers, should be addressed both deeply and cautiously. As a social services officer, I can only do one thing: determine whether aid should be given. However, if it is possible to proceed as a social worker, I can go deeper into the issues. In this regard, there are no academic qualifications for social services officers besides having a degree and passing a competitive examination. Therefore, we must develop the qualifications of social workers.

Chapter 6: Fostering Inter-ethnic Understanding Through the Sinhala and Tamil New Year Practice in Preschools

Chandima Jayasena
Department of Social Work
Pondicherry University

Tharindu Kasunpriya
The T.E.A. Project

Abstract: Ethnic disharmony remains a complex social problem in Sri Lanka. Various governmental and non-governmental organisations (NGOs) have implemented programmes to alleviate such tension. However, considering the country's current socio-economic-and political crisis, implementing long-term sustainable plans that address this issue is challenging. Therefore, this social work project applied practical activities to promote a better understanding of different ethnic groups in early childhood.

To achieve this objective, this project was implemented in two preschools, namely a rural Sinhala school belonging to the Dehiovita Divisional Secretariat in the Kegalle District and an international NGO (INGO)-led school for Tamil children from tea plantation communities in the Kandy district. The project involved 25 and 27 children from the Sinhala and Tamil preschools, respectively and six teachers from both schools. A holistic approach was used for early childhood development and two social workers carried out the project planning, implementation and follow-ups.

One of the important rituals in the country, the Sinhala and Tamil New Year practice (i.e. visiting relatives in the Sinhala *Negam Yama* ritual), was used as a social work activity to teach preschool children about other cultures, customs, Sinhala and Tamil food/clothing and religious locations and languages. The group activities were conducted using poems, storytelling and pictures, providing opportunities for active verbal and non-verbal interactions. An unexpected result of this project was understanding how parents and preschool

58

teachers can consistently offer primary and secondary socialisation for early childhood development.

Overall, this project was a new and exciting experience for parents and teachers of preschool children. Moreover, it changed their social attitudes, eliminated mistrust and built friendships between the ethnic groups, thus laying a foundation for peace.

Keywords: Ethnic understanding, Visiting relatives, Socialisation, Indigenous social work practice, Social work skills

Background and Aim

The theme of this study is ethnic disharmony, which remains a complex social issue in Sri Lanka. In this regard, various stakeholders, including the government sector and NGOs, have implemented programmes to alleviate such tension. In the current socio-economic-and political crisis in the country, implementing long-term sustainable plans that address this issue is a challenge. Thus, this social work project applied practical activities to promote better understanding between different ethnic groups in early childhood. Specifically, it used specific practical social work skills for Sri Lanka.

Ms Chandima Jayasena (the co-presenter) is a former NISD lecturer who is currently working on her PhD in India. As a social work educator and practitioner, she diligently maintains ongoing connections with former students who have completed their BSW. Moreover, she actively tracks their professional growth and explores possible collaborative opportunities for mutual benefit.

This project began after she met with former students, including myself. Although I had not connected with her at school, she saw what former students had done in the field. Subsequently, she suggested integrating our skills into practice and connecting the faculty members of the NISD with practitioners in the field. This project is one of the outcomes of this integration.

Regarding my background, my name is Tharindu Kasunpriya and I am currently working for an international NGO (INGO) called the T.E.A. Project. It is a registered charity and children's rights organisation in the UK located in Hanthana. I completed my BSW at the NISD and I am currently working on my MSW at the University of Peradeniya. I believe cultivating professional relationships with former students and teachers is essential.

The T.E.A. Project

The T.E.A. (Training, Empowerment and Awareness) Project was established in 2014, as a charity organisation that focuses on children's rights. In 2019, it opened a dedicated Centre for Children's Empowerment in Hanthana. Currently, we conduct all of our activities in this centre. One of our missions is to uplift and empower Sri Lankan children living in impoverished conditions through a holistic approach. Since we cannot do this alone, it is important to gain the support of schools, parents, unemployed youth and adult community members, all of whom we ask questions and search for their actual needs.

Meanwhile, our social work initiatives include free preschool and empowerment training to develop children's life skills and self-confidence, after-school support to nurture their interests and a free daily food programme to address their hunger for better focus. A Saturday service programme is also offered to empower adults and unemployed youth in the community. It is an inclusive outreach commitment to all. In all instances, we provide support, regardless of their background, ethnicity or religion, which means that we consider and treat everybody as human beings. Moreover, we collaborate with grassroots NGOs, schools and orphanages, and we can see a relationship with the social work perspective. We mobilise the support of those stakeholders to sustain their capacities. Beyond providing immediate relief, the long-term objective of our organisation is to promote ambition and create a brighter and more equitable future for children in Sri Lanka. Since we started in 2014, we have trained thousands of children.

Use of Cultural Rituals in Practices

In this social work project in Kandy, the children were primarily from tea plantation communities, where their parents worked as tea pickers or daily paid labourers. It was implemented in two preschools: a rural Sinhala school belonging to the Dehiovita Divisional Secretariat in the Kegalle District and an INGO-led school, called Tiny T.E.A. Preschool, for Tamil children in the Kandy district. Overall, the project involved 25 and 27 children from the Sinhala and Tamil preschools, respectively and 6 teachers, 4 volunteers and approximately 50 parents.

In this project, a holistic approach has been applied to early childhood development. Children from Kegalle with Sinhala cultural backgrounds came to share their learning experiences with those from Hindu and Tamil cultural backgrounds in Hanthana. Organising some traditional Hindu and Tamil foods, we had the opportunity to experience their religious practices and what we learned in their preschools. Although both groups of children had never met each other, we were surprised to see such an engagement between the two groups. Moreover, we created an opportunity for them to learn more about one another, specifically focusing on their beliefs, culture, customs, traditional practices and language. We shared poems, stories and pictures, presented a movie and shared how they worked together in the past and why it is essential to learn them. The parents were also present, which was good, as they had some misconceptions about the other ethnic groups and their cultural practices. Therefore, it was a good time for stakeholders to experience the importance of observing how children engaged.

At this point, I want to highlight a particular aspect that I observed. We asked everyone to make a friend between the Ratnapura children and those of the Tiny T.E.A preschool. Then they held hands and went to the *kovil* (Hindu temple) for *puja* (a worship ritual) because we wanted them to experience Hindu religious practices. As they were heading to the *kovil*, a Sinhala-speaking child asked the Tamil-speaking child *'katavahanavaa'*, after which the latter said 'What?'. As they sat together, they still held hands and continued to talk, even though they did not understand one another. However, no one was

Photo 3 *An Inter-ethnic Programme*

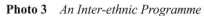

disturbed at the ceremony. This raises the following question. How can we integrate the practices of these children into our lives?

The following are some pictures of activities with teachers and children. In this case, we warmly welcomed them and shared different foods. We also allowed them to experience how tea estate communities are by presenting various aspects, such as the small canals.

Reflections of the Children, Parents and Teachers

According to children, parents and teachers, they stated the following: 'We met some new friends and their school is wonderful!'; 'We ate some delicious food and saw beautiful mountains' and 'We played together. We want to go again!'. Furthermore, parents said, 'We have never experienced this in our preschools!', while teachers said: 'Since the children are our future, the Sinhala-Tamil relationship is really important in Sri Lankan society'.

Challenges and Suggestions for Social Work

Since collaboration is essential for sustainability, we should advocate for the supervision of projects and establish relationships with students. In this regard, through the NISD, we have gained field-level experience, research experience and community development practices. If former students are in the field, they should also practice what they have learned, even though they are not officially 'social workers'. Regarding the challenge of dependency in Sri Lankan society, social workers must critically discuss theories rooted in the Western world in the local context to implement effective interventions. Moreover, I suggest that such dependent individuals be involved in the decision-making process and allow them to discover their hidden potential.

Finally, it is crucial to continue to empower children and promote their education by letting them think about their dependency and understand their hidden potential. At this point, what are the challenges that I may face? Should I do this or should I use my skills? Some community members say, 'We cannot do a job, so please give us something'. This can be difficult considering that some mothers and fathers both work, placing pressure on the children to take care of the younger ones. In this case, what do we say? How are they surviving?

Some possibilities include giving them initial capital to develop and grow or using existing services or NGOs. Thus, they can give back to society when they reach a certain age or standard. As additional recommendations, the integration of local knowledge to improve social work practices is required for relevant interventions. This is how we should think as social workers.

Conclusion

Overall, more social workers are needed in Sri Lanka. I also emphasise the significance of improving theoretical, educational and practical field experiences and advocate for the recognition of social work as a formal discipline in the country. Since hundreds of social workers graduate each year, I wonder how many students are active in the field and/or teaching at the NISD. As a social work graduate, I also wonder if they had the opportunity to become a lecturer at school. We must continue to think about the future of this field and recognise those that excel in such important endeavours.

Discussion with the Floor

Participant: You addressed the ethnic gap and it is fascinating. When we focus on the school syllabus for the children, they will go through it and say, 'This is *idli*' and 'This is milk rice', which are very practical. However, they can see the ethnicity gap.

Another Participant: What is the duration of this project? Can you carry out this type of project in a community without any external funding, but with community support?

Tharindu: We simply wanted to pilot the project. However, we need funding to sustain the organisation and hire experts to establish similar projects in other communities. Here is where we are at right now in the process. I hope projects like this are implemented on a larger scale so that more people can see the value of empowering children and reducing the ethnicity gap. However, it is a challenge. This is because it is not a 1-day or short-term project, but a long-term objective in which we must constantly adjust our procedures and structures. I feel fortunate to have the freedom to perform my duties as a social worker with the authority to integrate students, work with communities and develop various programmes. We are also optimistic because the founders of our organisation are from the United Kingdom and they have the knowledge and experience of working with children in that country.

Chapter 7: Youth Empowerment Through Volunteer-Based Community Development

R.M.H. Yasintha Rathnayake
Independent practitioner

Abstract: Sri Lankan youth are suffering from various types of unrest related to education, employment and health, mainly due to the consequences of the COVID-19 pandemic and the prevailing economic and political crisis. This situation has created psycho-social problems among young people such as substance abuse, mental illness and other health issues. Therefore, it is crucial to determine whether volunteer-based community development can be used as an effective strategy to empower youth to examine volunteerism and explore social work's role in this scenario. Special consideration is given to the nature of the tendency to volunteer, as part of the rich culture of Sri Lanka and the role that social work can play in interconnecting formal and informal volunteerism.

Therefore, I have applied the strength-based approach to volunteerism-based community development, both personally and professionally, by partnering with various local and international organisations. Specifically, I have implemented this strategy to form volunteer groups in communities, empower them through training to interact with different groups, such as vulnerable and neglected ones and help them become independent and responsible citizens.

My theme, empowerment of youth through volunteer-based community development in Sri Lanka, is based on a study conducted in the Bandaragama Division of the Kalutara District, which is affiliated with the youth volunteerism movement of the National Youth Services Council. This study is qualitative in nature and is based on primary data collected through the experiences of volunteers and their supervisors and secondary data from different sources of information.

The study findings provided information on the role of social work, government bodies and volunteer organisations in facilitating a healthy volunteering experience and the possibility of using volunteering as a standardised youth development strategy for their empowerment. My proposed model for youth empowerment based on volunteerism adopted theories/concepts from positive youth development and Rothman's locality development model. However, the critical consideration was localising the social work concepts in a culturally and contextually appropriate manner to Sri Lanka and focusing on the role of social work in bridging these areas of youth empowerment through volunteer involvement in community development.

Keywords: Youth, Volunteerism, Community development, Social work interventions

Background and Aim

I will examine the impact of community development and volunteerism on youth empowerment. My presentation is predominantly based on my MSW research at the NISD and my work experience. Overall, the content covers the social background of volunteering, my personal and practice background and my experiences through case studies.

Regarding the background of this study, volunteerism is not a new concept in Sri Lanka (see also Chapter 2). It is ingrained within the community, based on our cultural interventions and practices; we have a considerable history of volunteering. However, I wanted to determine whether volunteer-based community development can be used as a strategy for youth empowerment, especially after the COVID-19 pandemic and during the ongoing multi-dimensional economic crisis. In addition, I wanted to explore the role of social work in bringing this strategy into the classroom.

Volunteerism predominantly includes two dimensions, namely managed and unmanaged volunteers. Managed volunteers come from professions such as social workers and doctors, while unmanaged volunteers focus on charitable concepts for the community. I believe that managed and unmanaged volunteers are equally essential. However, there seems to be a gap between these two dimensions. Therefore, as a social worker, I also wanted to determine whether they could be connected through social work interventions.

Due to my experience of more than 10 years, young people have asked me why they should volunteer and what the benefits are. Hence, I identify the motivational factors for youth empowerment through volunteer-based community development and explore possible solutions for improvement in this study.

Personal and Practice Background

Regarding my background, I have worked as a volunteer case worker for Save the Children Sri Lanka. I have also contributed to the Vimuktha Global Foundation, a mental health organisation in Bangalore, India. Overall, I have been helping Sri Lanka Volunteers for approximately 19 years. Regarding my academic background, I received my MSW from NISD, focusing on youth development and organisational management. I am also pursuing a postgraduate counselling and psycho-social diploma at the University of Colombo, with practical work in the city of Colombo and its surrounding areas. I found that this combination of studies can also contribute to the field of social work. I will also share some experiences from when I practiced case management in the city of Colombo and its surrounding areas. I believe that this is the heart of social work.

I have also been involved in a project conducted by UNICEF due to the ongoing economic crisis. Specifically, this project provides psycho-social support to families and children, including those with vulnerable conditions under multidimensional crisis. I used case management to reach them. It also facilitates group-sized social support, especially for parents and caregivers.

My main case study was conducted at the Bandaragama Regional Board of the Youth Club. In Sri Lanka, youth clubs under the National Youth Services Council, from the ground level to the national level, include a mechanism for youth to participate in volunteer activities and skills development.

68

Photo 4 *Facilitating Group Psycho-social Support for Children*

Policy Initiatives to Address the Problems in the Community

In my attempt to address youth unrest and observe volunteerism as an effective process, I examined the National Youth Services Policy to see the corresponding interventions. In other words, we cannot motivate the youth simply by lecturing them. Instead, the activities must be fun, enjoyable and leisurely. Thus, I included such activities, while considering their health and well-being, since mental health issues have increased significantly during the ongoing crisis.

Collaborative Activities

Considering these matters, I organised some collaborative activities (e.g. leadership training, group counselling, etc.) with youth services officers, child probation officers and other stakeholders in the community. I also encouraged youth to contribute to small community intervention projects during their leisure time. The COVID-19 pandemic caused academic, economic and other related problems. Meanwhile, Sri Lanka has been experiencing a significant economic crisis, which has worsened the situation. Thus, these activities were specifically organised for the youth in this community.

Photo 5   *Group Activities by Youth*

Case Study

I also conducted interviews and observations using a qualitative study design. Overall, I categorised the volunteering experiences into two types: 1) empowerment factors; and 2) acceptance, support and recognition. Regarding the empowerment factors, many of the youth started talking about their feelings of self-recognition. They also realised their own capabilities, since they could not explore their hidden skills or potential in the current education system. Regarding a path for career development, a young man had yet to learn how to become a good trainer and felt trapped in an administrative job. However, through my interventions, he is now becoming a teacher and trainer in the community.

In particular, such interventions are a 'way out' of harmful social infractions, such as drug abuse, which is rampant among youth. The current environment itself may make them easily addicted to those kinds of harmful infractions. They mentioned that volunteering has been a major support to avoid such aspects. This module was developed through this practical study.

Overall, this case study focused predominantly on the personal and behavioural development and empowerment of youth in the community. Regarding their career development, the young people felt ready to take responsibility and become significant contributors to the country's national development. Moreover, as a multi-cultural, multi-religious country, they understood the importance of ethnic harmony, collaboration and positive influences. As part of their behavioural development, they understood the role of good leadership and positive community engagement while being friendly and cautious with the neighbourhood.

Conclusion

Based on the findings, volunteering can empower young people and increase their motivation to become independent and responsible citizens. For example, government-sponsored volunteerism and national recognition can increase their motivation to enter university. From the social work perspective, promoting their participation is essential at each implementation level.

Regarding Sri Lankan keywords in social work, volunteer work is called *swechcha sewaya* and *swechcha sanwidhana*. However, when we talk about everyday social work, it is yet to be recognised as a professional development. Social work could play an essential role in mediating all systems together. Social work has often been misinterpreted as 'charity work', rather than a professional field. Modules based on Western-rooted professional social work can be applied; however, we must customise them or develop our practices for Sri Lankan society. For example, I had to adapt my approach to the needs of the community specifically. In conclusion, social work can significantly bridge the gap between managed and unmanaged volunteerism, while volunteer-based community development can positively impact young people and their career development.

Discussion with the Floor

Participant: Numerous young people have reportedly developed addictions to various things, including social networks. What methods have you used to help them sign up for volunteer work?

Yasintha: I have used different strategies at the rural level, including an interactive activity. For example, I created a *shramadhaana* campaign that involved many people. In addition, if we offered a seminar, then only a few people would attend. Then we planned a volleyball match, after which a notice was distributed to everyone asking if they would like to participate in volunteer activities. Such examples show how we applied small techniques to inspire the greatest number of people. However, consistency is important.

Another participant: What challenges have you faced in the field?

Yasintha: One of the main challenges has been consistency. The other concerns parents' questions such as 'What makes volunteering worthwhile?' and 'What are the benefits?' Girls, in particular, experience difficulties. In other words, society does not recognise volunteering as a means of developing skills. Then some problems arise. We must meet with the parents because we should have known about it earlier. For example, sometimes only five or six people show up when the activities have been scheduled for 10 people. In this case, we have to call their parents for permission or personally visit them to give the impression that we are responsible. These are the ongoing methods that we employ.

Another participant: Who is most interested in volunteer activities? The boys or girls?

Yasintha: Although there is a certain stigma at the ground level, I think people no longer seem to care about it. However, girls tend to enjoy these activities more than boys.

Another participant: Can we inspire more young people to participate in volunteer activities, considering the economic crisis and the competitive educational system? What obstacles do volunteer social workers face?

Yasintha: Recognition at the national level is essential. I believe that volunteerism should be promoted on a national scale. Approximately five years ago, there was an organisation called *yowun puraya* (යොවුන් පුරය) that adopted the concept of *yowun haula*. It was extremely successful.

Chapter 8: Incorporating Social Case Work Practice: Enhancing Individual Well-being Through Comprehensive Support

Vivetha Gunaretnam
Programme Officer
International Resource Development and Management
World Vision International

Abstract: This case study illustrated social workers' vital role in promoting the safety and well-being of vulnerable populations in the Sri Lankan context. Thus, the background of the case work, as well as extensive experience and knowledge of social work and related fields, were used effectively to identify the complex needs of the family and tailor a culturally sensitive approach that was appropriate for the Sri Lankan context. The case worker also recognised the importance of understanding and respecting the cultural values and norms of the Sri Lankan community and its impact on the family's response to the intervention. This included providing culturally appropriate care that respected family values and beliefs while ensuring children's safety and well-being. Furthermore, the case worker prioritised ethical considerations throughout the intervention, including confidentiality, informed consent and client autonomy, established a strong relationship with the family and collaborated with other service providers to develop a comprehensive and coordinated care plan. Overall, the findings offer a compelling argument for the importance of social workers in the lives of their clients and families and they emphasise the importance of applying culturally sensitive approaches and multiple theoretical models to provide comprehensive support that addresses the client's complex needs.

Keywords: Cultural competency, Child sexual abuse, Crisis intervention, Advocacy, Client-centred approach; நேரம்/ காலம் சரி இல்லை, சூனியம், ஏழரை சனி, சாத்திரம் பார்ப்பவர், அருட்தந்தை

Background

Regarding my background, I am currently pursuing an MSW at the NISD and a Master's in Human Rights at the University of Colombo. I previously obtained a BSW and a Diploma in Counselling from the NISD. I currently serve as a programme officer at World Vision, an international NGO, where I connect development opportunities and grants with vulnerable populations, particularly children in Sri Lanka. My relevant training includes human rights, child protection, drug and alcohol addiction, leadership, project management and conflict resolution.

I will present my casework, which is not an actual intervention plan, but an analysis of a Tamil-speaking community from a social work perspective. Social workers must understand the attitudes and related aspects of the community. I selected the location of my casework from the Batticaloa District, a community with 260 households. Their primary livelihood is fishing, while others go to daily work and some small businesses such as grocery stores and meat shops. Meanwhile, the predominant religion is Christianity and most are Tamil-speaking. The critical stakeholders in this community include fisheries, the local government and private NGOs.

Case Description[2]

As shown in the genogram of the case in Figure 2, there is the father who suffers from alcoholism and drug abuse (represented by the square) and the mother who has diabetes (represented by the circle). They have two daughters, one of whom is my 15-year-old client and the other who is 30 years of age and married. In this case throughout my previous organisation, my client had been sexually abused (groomed) by her brother-in-law.

Based on my previous social work experience with this family, the relationship between my client and the brother-in-law was always dysfunctional and broken. From the point of view of my client's mother, there was always a conflict, as indicated by the jagged lines in the figure. The main problem was that my client was vulnerable to being abused by her brother-in-law due to

---

2) Some case details and other information have been changed to protect the anonymity of those involved.

the family situation. For example, father's lack of income negatively affected mother's illness, which, in turn, affected my client's behaviour and depression, leaving her vulnerable to brother-in-law sexual abuse.

Figure 2   *Genogram of the Case*

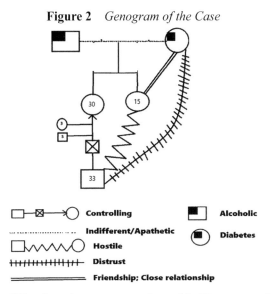

Note: This differs from the genogram style used in Western-rooted research and practice (see the description in the text).

Background of the Community

This case occurred in an eastern province fishing community, including some unique cultural practices and church-centred activities. For example, people in the area celebrate the Easter and Christmas festivals. In addition, they maintain strong community relationships. In some instances, community members take care of other families. For example, the neighbour's relationship with my client's family included sharing food, gossiping and becoming personally involved in family conflicts.

Engaging in the lives of extended families is common in the eastern and northern provinces, including the ritual of the groom going to the bride's family after marriage. These common practices enable a particular community to accept their new arrival: they always have good fortune, like going somewhere before things, seeing the appropriate time and wearing traditional clothing.

In this sense, when someone wears black, it indicates some level of sadness or misfortune. The practice of black magic is also commonly known to everyone. For example, when a particular family faces an unfortunate event, then they (before considering the objective reasons for the problem) tend to blame similar past events. They also rely on traditional healers such as fortune tellers and the church priest. Whenever things happen, they often go to horoscope. If fortune tellers mention something ominous, they tend to focus on this aspect and continue their lives accordingly.

Another common characteristic of the community is related to its traditional beliefs. This community celebrated unique functions, for example, the puberty ceremony, inviting numerous people.

Other significant beliefs and traditions include active church participation, a strong belief in the paranormal and supernatural (e.g. black magic and bad omens) and exceptional hospitality. Regarding the latter, if a visitor does not accept tea or water, a host perceives it as a refusal of welcome.

Experience and Practical Skills in Understanding the Community Perspective

My client was sexually abused twice by her brother-in-law. As a child protection worker, I immediately took action on this case. Although we successfully developed an intervention plan, the following questions had to be analysed from the community point of view.

The first aspect was traditional gender roles. Regarding breadwinners, we tend to choose the father, the brother-in-law or some other male family member. Being a breadwinner indicates that this person leads the family financially. In this particular case, the brother-in-law was the breadwinner because of the alcoholic father. This situation allowed the brother-in-law to continue living with the family (even after marriage), contributing to the problem.

The second aspect was the silencing of the girl. Speaking about their experiences was likely taboo in the community. Deep-rooted attitudes discourage girls from sharing their experiences, particularly regarding sex, sexual abuse and grooming. However, when a girl is reluctant to talk about the sexual behaviours of others, the risk of being abused increases. Thus, these customs might have influenced the abusive behaviour of the brother-in-law.

The third aspect was the subjective acceptance by the community of alcohol abuse. Most of the breadwinners were not occasional drinkers, but had alcohol problems. Therefore, when my client talked about her father's alcoholic behaviour, many people said, 'My father is also the breadwinner and he drinks alcohol'. This acceptance probably led to the father's indifference, affecting the vulnerability of his child.

The fourth was superstitions and beliefs. In this sense, my client's mother strongly believed in bad omens and spirits. This also paved the way for silencing my client when the brother-in-law abused her. For example, my client's mother simply went to the fortune teller when something happened. This misguided trust in fortune and horoscopes deterred the mother from taking action on the issue. In summary, these community attitudes played a significant role in exacerbating my client's problem. In other words, these components increased the client's vulnerability.

Dealing with this Issue in the Field

To address this issue, the key intervention was to contact a child rights protection officer (CRPO), who immediately separated the brother-in-law and the child. This intervention also included the empowerment of the community resource (e.g. the church priest and the horoscope/fortune teller) to change the father's behaviour. This approach emphasised the use of community resources and support networks to effectively address the situation. This effort was instrumental in garnering support and enhancing the mental well-being of both the family and the client. Currently, the father has managed to control his alcoholic habit.

Skills and Experiences

Overall, this practice advanced my analytical skills. Specifically, I had to analyse all components at the community and individual levels. Regarding the latter, I focused on how the behaviour and attitude of the mother influenced the child's well-being. As for the community level, I had to consider community desensitisation, which proved difficult, since I could not directly confront the community members. I would have been excluded from further discussions and actions if I did. Thus, I had to apply the following skills as a social worker. This included effective networking to strengthen the capacity to mobilise support and resources; strategic and confrontational communication to ensure effective message delivery, especially when confronting sensitive issues; local cultural proficiency to deeply understand local practices, beliefs and attitudes; research skills to enable evidence-based decision-making; adaptation and acceptance and cultural knowledge to promote cultural sensitivity and respect.

Challenges

How are cultures, traditions and beliefs analysed? In this context, I faced three main challenges. The first was the limitations of confrontation. In my casework, one of the key challenges was the difficulty in initiating confrontations with the family. The approach aimed to address sensitive issues without causing offence. This required careful navigation. In the case of the client's mother, especially when the horoscope teller mentioned something in a certain way, she always confronted and reverted some answers. We had to deal with the mother's habit of following the advice of the fortune teller, her strong beliefs about cultural traditions and her attitude towards her daughter.

The second challenge was the effort to convince the family of the logical steps and the necessary changes to address the situation. This process demanded patience, empathy and strategic communication.

The third challenge was my personal growth and acceptance. Specifically, I struggled to accept and understand the attitudes and practices of certain family members. In fact, it took several moments of self-reflection to reach a point of acceptance. However, after such introspection and a better understanding of the community, I adapted to the situation.

Recommendations

My recommendations to social workers in Sri Lanka are as follows. First, while developing a programme and activities with a client, tailoring them to the community is crucial to achieve the intended outcomes. This includes adapting strategies to the cultural and individual needs of the community.

Second, a hybrid approach is imperative. There are various approaches to social casework, none of which guarantees a positive outcome. For example, Sri Lankan social work should carefully combine elements from both Western and traditional practices, while recognising the value of diversity and inclusivity. When combining these two approaches, one must always be prepared to develop creative and innovative solutions.

Third, a paradoxical intervention technique can be used. It is a notable approach in psychology where therapists work with clients to transform their beliefs and attitudes. This can also be applied in social work, especially in the Sri Lankan context. In this regard, I want to emphasise the importance of harmonising Western-rooted theories with Sri Lankan traditions and beliefs to facilitate effective social work within this culturally diverse nation.

Chapter 9: Harnessing and Optimising Fieldwork Through Indigenous Supervision: A Reflective and Reflexive Approach

Varathagowry Vasudevan
National Institute of Social Development

Abstract: This study examines how supervision of social work practice is perceived in the field to improve the practical aptitude, attitudes and skills of students in community work, as part of the requirements for the diploma, bachelor and master in social work. I believe that supervision is a supportive, mutual relationship in which students apply the concepts learned in classrooms to the field and trained supervisors conduct on-site visits, individual conferences and regular meetings to improve/optimise their skills development in community work. In general, practice supervision aims to improve and optimise student learning in community work through a transformation process. In this regard, this study focuses on the personal journey of a social worker educator, based on reflective and reflexive accounts of applied supervision practices that aim to prepare social workers for the field. It also includes a critical reflection on how indigenous practices are being overlooked and how Westernised supervision practices are being promoted to address the complexity of social work in the Sri Lankan context. In addition, it promotes integrated supervision practices to enable the Sri Lankan community's unique transformation towards achieving sustainable development goals.

Keywords: Social work education, Fieldwork education, Indigenous and local knowledge

Challenges in Social Work Practice Supervision

Based on my experience as field supervisor for social work students in Sri Lanka, I believe that self-reflective and reflexive critical analysis should be carried out to explore the supervision of students' community social work. Both supervisors and supervisees can apply this during the six months of fieldwork for diploma (including community-level mobilisation and its contribution), bachelor's (including community-level issues to facilitate community and organisational changes) and master's (including community-level policy practices and changing existing policies in Sri Lanka) in social work.

According to the findings of my research-based practice, the reflective process of field supervision can result in the erosion of indigenous approaches to collaborative supervision. These indigenous supervisory practices include faculty field supervisor liaisons with agencies and students, on-site supervision to address innate issues such as faculty field visits for community engagement, residential workshops for reviewing the field progress of all students and faculty field visits to receive open feedback from students. These supervision strategies and activities are intended as a holistic approach to prepare social workers for integrated community development in Sri Lanka. In particular, such supervisory relationships are not for students and junior/senior social work faculty members to maximise their skills development. As for indigenous supervision practices, integrating theory, skills, attitudes and mindsets is crucial to perceive contextual practices for making differences and understanding which role models of fieldwork supervision can be effectively promoted and practiced. This may shed light on the value and benefits of supervisory models in this context, which have yet to be fully examined.

Overview of Social Work Education in Sri Lanka

Based on this background, describing my reflection of fieldwork supervision in social work education is imperative (See Introduction in this book). Professional social work education in Sri Lanka began in 1952 with the establishment of the Ceylon Institute of Social Work. This institute conducted short-term training for welfare personnel and eventually developed a 1-year certificate programme in social work. In 1965, the school launched a two-year diploma programme in social work. To provide higher education in social work, the school was upgraded and renamed the NISD in 1992. In 2005, this institute was recognised as a degree-awarding institution by the government based on the recommendation of the UGC.

Today, the Sri Lanka School of Social Work, a division of this institute, provides professional social work education in Sri Lanka. The two-year diploma and four-year BSW programmes produce basic social workers, while the MSW programme, introduced in 2008, develops managerially competent practitioners. All three programmes include extensive supervised fieldwork with individuals, families, social groups and communities. Meanwhile, the NISD training division, regular social work programmes, part-time and outreach diploma programmes in social work and other related subject areas include supervised fieldwork. However, despite NISD increasing the number of intakes in its programmes and social work education being a well-recognised and popular discipline in universities worldwide, Sri Lanka is yet to gain such professional recognition, even though our degrees are in line with global standards.

Supervision Practices in Social Work Field Education

In general, field education in social work is integrated learning and teaching in which social work students have opportunities to learn by performing activities in a complex social context. Thus, the knowledge and skills acquired in the classroom are applied to concrete actions for facilitating social development and working with individuals, families, groups, organisations and communities. Fieldwork is also an opportunity for social work students to advocate for restructuring structures and systems through evidence-based research, social administration and policy practices.

According to the Global Standard of Social Work Education and Training (IASSW & IFSW., 2020), the adverse effects of colonisation and educational imperialism are evident in the development of social work in the global South. I strongly believe that without critical examinations of their suitability and potential effectiveness in local contexts, the theoretical perspectives, practice methods, techniques and skills developed in the Global North should not be transferred to the global South. Thus, this reflective study examines the supervision practices of social work field education in Sri Lanka. Moreover, it critically examines community work field placement and its supervision practices.

Community work for community development is one of the field placements in social work education. It consists of the steps of the community organisation process for community development.

Personal Background

Regarding my background, I have a bachelor's degree in sociology (University of Jaffna), a postgraduate diploma in applied sociology (University of Colombo), a master's degree in social work, with a specialisation in family and child welfare (Tata Institute of Social Sciences, Mumbai, India) and a master's degree in public management (Sri Lanka Institute of Development Administration). I have also completed a 1-year certificate course in teaching higher education (University of Colombo). Thus, I believe that I am fully qualified as a social work educator with experience in supervision practice, training and research.

Applied Skills in My Current Social Work Supervision Practice

As part of field education in social work and as a supervision tool, I introduced reflective journal writing to both undergraduate and postgraduate field education programmes at the School of Social Work in Sri Lanka. My social work supervision practice generally begins with the students to facilitate self-supervision, together with reflective learning, peer supervision, face-to-face supervision and group supervision. However, collaborations with field supervisors, agency facilitators and students, and on-site student and community engagement and feedback, are still under-utilised. My supervision practices include alternative telephonic supervision methods through computer technology and social media. This has been especially helpful in the field supervision of students in vulnerable communities. Thus, fieldwork is the process of co-learning a complex situation by facilitating field supervision.

Social Work Perspectives of Indigenous and Westernised Supervision Practices

As a social work educator and supervisor, my reflection on localised supervision with structured educational, personal and administrative functions has revealed several gaps in this process. Such gaps include the lack of sufficient benchmarks for social worker skills and the difficulty of systematically assessing the level of skills development during fieldwork. Similarly, from the fieldwork perspective, the students could not transform community engagement opportunities into concrete actions due to the loss of collaborations with community volunteers. Then community participation, such as collaborative work with stakeholders who volunteered for common community needs and fulfilled themselves with their willpower, was primarily facilitated through faculty and field supervisors.

Generally, field supervisors perform field visits, home visits and on-site supervision, in addition to organisational supervision. This threefold approach is used due to the dearth of practice supervisors within organisations. Meanwhile, recent budget restrictions further challenge and constrain these practices.

Despite a reasonable cost for conducting a social work programme, its benefits to students are learning, community change and understanding the reality of certain situations. The supporting organisation also benefits from their involvement. Furthermore, the practices of student social workers are highly valued when considering their future employment and potential. Hence, the NISD and its outcome-based higher education can result in a win–win situation, wherein students, field agencies and social work education all benefit.

Although social work is professional-paid work in general, my mindset revolves around student volunteerism and an integrated, holistic community development-based process. My experiences in skill supervision have also identified the following gaps between the education of the social work field and the perceived need to be a community catalyst to facilitate the community organisation process and community development. Then, I faced issues that critically reflected gaps in addressing field practice.

1. Lack of critical reflections on intersectionality, citizenship and policy practices, with evidence-based indigenous knowledge integration for community socioeconomic revitalisation
2. Issues regarding the integration of Westernised social work theory

into fieldwork and the use of field journals to promote the practice knowledge of students at the bachelor and master levels

3. Challenge of coordinating various stakeholders while conducting fieldwork by students

4. Although various improvements have been made at the level of the educational programme, the availability of practice supervisors and the creation of fieldwork units for coordination between stakeholders, administrative decision-making still does not necessarily include the promotion of community development.

Recommendations for Improving the Quality of Fieldwork Supervision

In this study, this relevant supervisory relationship defines and structures the wide range of student learning tasks and experiences. Contemporary research on social work education suggests that the value of this learning practice continues to be universally recognised (Shardlow & Doel, 1996). However, Cooper (2007) argued that field education can only occur during a one-on-one relationship between a student and supervisor and suggested that learning experiences may be reliant on the core tasks/roles of the organisation in which the student is expected to perform similarly to an employee.

In Sri Lanka, the absence of clinical models and the use of an integrated supervisory function with users, delivery officers, social work educators and fieldwork supervisors have worked to effectively prepare social workers in the community to make differences in employment, which indicates that when deprived of this collaborative support, students will 'squeeze in' between the three hierarchical levels (Tsui, 2004). Moreover, it suggests that the basis for the indigenous social work lies in field practice. Meanwhile, localising the concepts learned in a practical context can offer a greater understanding of the field setting and improve the ability of social work students to convert theory into practice. Therefore, developing the skills sets required for social work is possible and feasible.

Conclusions and Recommendations

Community work supervision practices were adapted to local culture, while integrating administrative, personal, supportive and educational tasks performed by social work students who could make a difference through community mobilisation. Meanwhile, working with individuals and groups was shaped by a community-based self-help approach that linked diverse welfare services, rather than putting pressure on determining how much a social work supervisor can oversee the community's transformation. My belief is that appropriate integration of localised or globalised practices is imperative. In this regard, evidence-based supervision models should continue to be used to transform student social workers, which in turn can have a positive impact on all Sri Lankan communities.

PART III:
DIALOGUE

Chapter 10: Exploring a Framework for Dialogue: Why Focus on Local and Foreign Knowledge in Social Work Practice?

Masateru Higashida
Asian Research Institute for International Social Work
Shukutoku University

Abstract: Local and indigenous knowledge has received increased attention in international discussions on social work, which may differ from mainstream Western-rooted theories. In fact, many scholars have stated that Western-rooted approaches are inappropriate in Asia due to different socio-cultural contexts. However, how can we explore such contextually relevant practices? Thus, this chapter explores the knowledge and skills in social work practice while critically discussing the relationship with foreign knowledge. I also focus on the relationship between local and indigenous knowledge and foreign knowledge in the practice of social work in Asia, based on my practical experiences. In this case, critical discussions are required regarding unilateral intervention from external sources. Moreover, I will discuss the importance of collaboration and dialogue among social workers based on practical and subjective experiences at the grassroots level.

Keywords: International social work, Indigenous social work, Asia, International development

Background[3]

The following dialogue is very experimental and I am excited to see what happens. Today, I will explore the knowledge and skills of social work practice in Sri Lanka while discussing the relationship with foreign/transnational knowledge. This chapter will follow a dialogue/discussion (Chapter 11).

Regarding my background, I worked as a social worker for two years in rural Sri Lanka. Throughout my career, sometimes practicing without the title of 'social worker', I have maintained a close relationship with social work.

Additionally, I mention the Asian Research Institute for International Social Work (ARIISW) to provide an institutional background because the theme of the theme of this session is related to this organisation. The ARIISW has focused on international and Buddhist social work since its establishment in 2016, led by Dr Tatsuru Akimoto, who is currently its Honorary Director and Guest Professor as of 2023; (Akimoto et al., 2020; Asian Research Institute for International Social Work, 2018). ARIISW has also been concerned about the hegemonic imposition of dominant social work frameworks, calling them 'Western-rooted professional social work' (Akimoto, 2017; Akimoto et al., 2020). Their assumption of Western-rooted professional social work is that practices by professional social workers and qualified professionals are primarily based on Western-rooted approaches, which would be reasonable if we discuss the theme within a specific range.

However, our various projects have found cases that do not fit the dominant discourse on social work professions, including Buddhist social work research (Akimoto et al., 2020; Higashida, 2023b). Thus, the ARIISW has promoted the international discussion of the meaning of social work for and with all people through ISW lends (Akimoto, 2024).

Episodes in the Field

Now, I will discuss two episodes that represent today's theme. When I worked in rural Sri Lanka, I participated in practices with locals I had never

---

3) Part of this chapter is based on the author's previous work: Higashida, M. (2022). Indigenous, Foreign and Transnational Knowledges in Social Work Practice: Reinterpretation of the findings of qualitative studies on practitioners in Sri Lanka and Japan. Annual report of the Asian Research Institute for International Social Work, 6, 1-13. Chiba: Shukutoku University.

seen in my home country. When I first observed it, I immediately thought 'What is this?', as I could not understand the context and meaning of their activities.

For example, I witnessed a ground-breaking ceremony for establishing a workshop for people with disabilities, which included community mobilisation in a disability inclusion programme. This workshop was coordinated by government sector social services officers, whom I considered 'social workers'. Another example was the *sil samadan weema*, organised by social services officers (Higashida, 2016). Their practices often applied cultural and religious aspects and methods naturally and conventionally. Although such practices are most likely common for local practitioners, they are considered unique/ unknown to outsiders.

Brief Discussion

Various scholars have stated that Western-rooted approaches are often inappropriate in Asian countries/communities due to different contexts such as religious and cultural matters (Gray & Coates, 2010). However, sometimes their actual practices are unclear.

The usual aspects for practitioners in the local context may not be unique, but they are just common sense. However, it is sometimes difficult to identify common sense in a specific context. As an old saying in English goes, 'It is hard to see what is under your nose', which means that sometimes things are too close to see. As I explained earlier, perhaps local practices may not be unique for local practitioners but may be significant for others. Thus, I believe that it would be mutually beneficial to learn from each other. In other words, this experimental session explores the interactions between insiders and outsiders for facilitating the co-production of practical knowledge.

Process and Some Accounts[4]

I would also like to examine the overall process because it relates to this conference's dialogue. This practical and preliminary activity has been continuously implemented since 2021, after receiving approval from the Research Ethics Committee of the Aomori University of Health and Welfare on 26 May of that year (No. 21017). Subsequently, semi-structured interviews were conducted with six practitioners related to social work (Higashida et al., 2022). Consultations with stakeholders were also encouraged. The first face-to-face roundtable discussion for this project was held in January 2023, after two prior consultations were conducted remotely. Finally, discussions on this new practical dialogue were held after sharing the findings and plans.

The kick-off roundtable discussion to launch this project occurred at the NISD on 24 January 2023. This meeting was intended to enable social work practitioners to share rarely recorded experiences and explore socio-culturally relevant and practical knowledge. Furthermore, it was attended by 18 people, 7 of whom were practitioners. The session was coordinated by Dr Muhammad Ashker, with then-Additional Director General Mrs Shamini Attanayake delivering the opening remarks. Mr Amarawansa Ranaweera, then-President of SLAPSW, also delivered a speech before Higashida's keynote presentation on sharing practical knowledge. In addition, the participants discussed various issues related to the next conference.

Participants were divided into two groups for group discussions and members of each group were expected to share their experiences/opinions. These discussions highlighted the prevailing issues in Sri Lanka, ranging from individual to macrolevel social welfare concerns and identified a transition towards an individualistic society, especially in urban areas. For example, a participant pinpointed the changing context of social work as follows:

We are currently individualistic. So, social bonds tend to be weak. When we worked socially, we used to have togetherness and we intervened in a problem, even at the village level. However, now it is the other way around.

---

4) This section has been edited for reprint based on the editors' previous research: Higashida, M., Attanayake, S., Ranaweera, A., Ashker, M., & Kumara, R. (2023). Dialogue for reciprocal exchange of social work knowledge in Sri Lanka. Annual report of the Asian Research Institute for International Social Work, 7, 7-13. Chiba: Shukutoku University.

People only come forward looking for solutions after a problem occurs. In this way, our service delivery system has changed. [...] We still have some differences in culture. Therefore, we need to move forward in such aspects.

In the meeting, diverse social work issues were also discussed, including the inadequate understanding of social work as a profession. For example, some participants mentioned that the number of social workers remained small and that opportunities for their capacity building were lacking, indicating that increased research initiatives and increased awareness are crucial.

Some participants, especially researchers, highlighted the importance of indigenous knowledge and practices in the performance of social work while underscoring the significance of a collective and community-based approach. Moreover, a participant introduced a collective approach to poverty alleviation, citing Buddhist philosophy:

Buddhist philosophy, as indigenous knowledge, is fundamental in poverty alleviation. [...]. As shown in the Story of Maga Manawaka [Maga Manawaka Jathaka Kathawa], we must collectively resolve the issues faced by those who are in poverty-level situations. In fact, their situations were alleviated through the Samurdhi movement.

Another participant emphasised the importance of family-centred values as a backdrop to their practices, even during the country's transformation to an individualistic society:

Therefore, if we explore local and indigenous practices, then the value given to the family in the context of our cultural practices can be further strengthened through social work.

However, although time constraints made it difficult to achieve further substantive discussions, they were sometimes unintentionally directed towards Western-rooted social work discourses. Such divergences elucidated that it was paramount to establish and reinforce the themes of these discussions.

Indeed, Mr Ranaweera's comments to the presenters from other countries were illuminating when another international exchange (Session 9) was held online in Bangladesh on 12 May 2023:

We are adopting the Western model in our country [Sri Lanka] [...], but the people are unaware of the meaning of social work [...] As the scholars [in other countries] clearly stated, social work is not recognised as a profession in our country. [...] Our society is more community-oriented, in which we help one another. For example, if something happens in our neighbourhood, then we tell relatives and meet them. [...] We participate in their ceremonies and events as a family. [...] Thus, people do not understand the difference between this type of community action and social work.

This may be the main reason behind this lack of development of social work in our country. [...]. We have been promoting social work for more than 70 years, but it has yet to be adequately developed. Therefore, we must find our own ways to implement cultural-based practices and integrate them with social work in our country.

Finally, several implementation-related challenges have become clear. One such difficulty is related to the articulation of experiences by practitioners themselves. According to Mr Ranaweera, workshops have been held for social work practitioners in the past, but we must consider how such verbalisation and documentation can be accomplished in a manner familiar to practitioners. We believe this issue is also linked to how we can use outsiders' perspectives to examine common local events.

Chapter 11: Dialogue of Practices

Following the kick-off meeting on 24 January 2023 (see Chapter 10), this dialogue from the conference on 2 November 2023 was facilitated by Mr Amarawansa Ranaweera and Dr Masateru Higashida. A total of 35 practitioners and researchers[5] participated in this one-and-a-half-hour discussion, asking them to consider the following three points.

Q1. What are the key terms of your social work practices in a specific context, without necessarily using English terms?
Q2. Why do you think these perspectives are essential?
Q3. What do you think about the roots of these terms and/or perspectives? (e.g. the West, home country or others?)

It is important to note that the participants' accounts are not based on evidence but on their personal (and sometimes contrasting) views/opinions. However, they are included here because they are still useful for discussion.

Open Discussion

Exploring socio-culturally relevant concepts

Piyumanthi: A discussion was held on 30 November 2023 in the Grama Niladhari division, with Dr Higashida in attendance. At that time, I contacted several social service agencies and talked about social work tailored to our culture. Currently, we use a European concept that is, a concept rooted in the West. Meanwhile, he asked how to perform social work based on our traditional customs such as agriculture. For example, volunteering, which is called *attam kramaya* (අත්තම් ක්‍රමය), might be

---

5) Their narratives, some of which were in Sinhalese and Tamil, were summarised and edited by the editors. Some of the participants' names were excluded to protect their anonymity.

considered social work in our country. It was often done in the past, even though it is not the basis for its consideration as a profession. Because we do not have a specific practice model, we have talked about Western-rooted social work and developed it. Thus, this dialogue introduces a unique social work system to our country. We need to follow up on our cultural events. To do so, we also need to go back approximately 200 years and conduct an extensive study on how we have dealt with the cultural elements of our country.

As stated above, the consensus of our discussion was that we must create a concept of social work that is compatible with our culture; then we discussed it for two hours at the meeting. Accordingly, we covered various areas, such as the police, social service officers and MOH. When the social services officer with the background of agricultural services commented on his field, he stated that we must determine if social work can be related to the agricultural development. Even though we are now limited to certain matters, old community work system is called social work. Furthermore, a revisiting of this issue in the future was considered necessary.

Asmiyas: We can also use an indigenous approach to develop a village-level community. There is a term in Sinhala; however, it is related to the social work profession. What are the negative impacts on the village? Currently, the problem of dengue seems to be the subject of focus. To remove this disease, we must clean our village by *shramadaana.*

Piyumanthi: *Shramadaana* is what we currently use in participatory development. This term is present in our country and culture. Nevertheless, now, we tend to use another concept, participatory development. However, such development is what our country needs.

Asmiyas: You mentioned *attam* (අත්තම) and *kayiya* (කයිය) right? Are these considered participatory development?

Kumudu Wedisinghe: When I was involved with the rural development training institute, they called their basic concept 'the *mutagen* approach', similar to the social work concept. Meanwhile, in Sinhala, they used the term *viparyaasa kaaraka* (විපර්යාස කාරක).

Eron: As Mr Asmiyas stated, *shramadaana* has a relationship with social work, having some traditional values. The concept basically means 'alms-giving'. Specifically, the word *shramadaana* (ශ්‍රමදාන) ends with the word *daana* (දාන) or *daanaya* (දානය), which is sacred in the Sri Lankan religious culture; it means giving to any human being. Thus, regarding social empowerment, we include the word *shrama* (ශ්‍ර) to form *shramadana*; then a change occurred at the village level. Although the concept of alms-giving is currently applied to participatory development in some locations, it has also become a symbol of marginalisation in some places. For example, giving alms to the elderly or children can have a negative impact on their self-esteem and dignity.

Meanwhile, scholars in social work have discussed the so-called empowering mode. What does this mean? Regardless of age, one should be empowered in their life. As mentioned earlier, servants are assumed in alms-giving. Servant means that they get something; before that, they worship the Buddha, pray and give alms as much as it appears to be a kind act, but these may decrease others' self-esteem. Those people give merit. However, we have converted that alms-giving concept. In other words, it does not empower them. Social workers tend to promote giving alms, especially to disabled people, indicating that disabled people are considered to have nothing to do. This paradox is something social workers should keep in mind and critically discuss.

In addition, we started to limit some aspects to using English terms in Sri Lankan culture such as 'caste marginalisation'. This English term in this culture could refer to marginalisation or empowerment. Regarding the latter, even if an individual is in a lower caste, it can sometimes be empowering, depending on the circumstances. However, we tend to group them as marginalised people using English terms. It should be noted that the English term 'marginalisation' is often used to introduce the caste system. However, it is not necessarily marginalisation in the Sri Lankan context. In this sense, applying the local context when interpreting people's skills and identities is important, without considering academic theories or thinking.

Hariharathamotharan: I would like to emphasise the importance of incorporating traditional practices into social work in the Sri Lankan context. For example, Hinduism includes traditional practices that promote individuals' psychological and social well-being, while Christianity has its own customs. Meanwhile, Buddhists in some southern areas perform the *daha ata sanniya* or *thovil* dance. In this dance, there are different *sanniyas*; each with its own practices such as *wedi sanniya* and *deva sanniya*. Many people performed this activity for the latter, even during the COVID-19 pandemic. Despite the differences, every religion has its own practices,

100

all empowering people in certain ways. Therefore, social workers must recognise such practices. For example, in regard to Islam, there are specific passages the Koran. Thus, every religion includes its own practices. Naturally, this empowers people to enhance their well-being.

Nilupuli Nayanthara: I work as a community worker in a fishing village called Siriwardhana Pedesa, where 90% of the population is Catholic. Interestingly, it includes a social support system in which the Father of the Church visits every house on the island. Currently, the island includes approximately 3,000 houses, with two or three families per house. It is amazing that a person like him can do that every day. Specifically, he walks down the lanes every evening, visits their houses and talks to the people. I do not know the exact name or concept of such activities, but he seems like a change agent.

Since I could not make such visits, I would simply ask him, 'Father, what is happening in this house?' After that, he told me everything. Through his approach, he could connect families with other families and relevant organisations in times of need and financial distress. Within the community, families and organisations were tremendously supportive. In some cases, they would provide jobs, money and clothing, among others.

In another instance, I read English stories and performed various activities for a class of approximately 50 students. Due to the high dropout rate, parents and families were grateful for my efforts. In some cases, they felt that I was 'sent by God' to serve the community. I am unsure whether I had a positive or negative impact, but at the time, I certainly made a difference.

Relationship with the Western-rooted concepts

Female 1: I have an experience that I would like to share. When I started my master's degree in social work, it was a new discipline for me. At the end of my fieldwork, I was able to work in palliative care settings. 'When I completed my graduate studies, I left India and returned to Sri Lanka, where I started a unit in the Mattakkuliya area for comprehensive community-based palliative care. We had a trained doctor and nurse, while my friend and I served as trained social workers. Although this unit eventually closed, our practice was based on the Western-rooted model. You may wonder why I am sharing this experience. I believe that combining various aspects of the Western model with our cultural context can develop a suitable model for localisation of the community.

Hariharathamotharan: Regardless of the Sri Lankan context, we all have Westernised ideologies that we apply in our teaching. For example, although we have mentioned the IFSW/IASSW's (2014) Global Definition of the Social Work Profession, when I attended a conference in Tanzania, they did not discuss the definition of social work. This indicates that when you become a social worker in Tanzania, others will not consider whether you have indigenous practice or experience in social work, as it is 'both sides of the same coin'. Hence, they developed a hybrid mixture of explanatory models. In Sri Lanka, we have done this by mixing our culture with Westernised ideologies. However, we do not discuss these issues in indigenous or religious practice.

I have also worked with some of these traditional leaders who promote psychological-social well-being for members of their community. However, some people strictly follow a specific belief system. When we met our clients, they expected us to understand this system. As a social worker, how can we improve your well-being? Thus, we must use a holistic approach in actual situations to motivate people to understand evidence based on practice.

A case of mental health activities with traditional social systems

Asanka: I work at the General Hospital in Peradeniya, where my focus is on people with mental health disorders. In one ward, approximately 10 inpatients (mostly university students) had recently attempted suicide. In this case, everyone, including the surrounding community, knew that the people in this ward had some problems. When we attended a case conference, the people in the village said that they knew that he/she had problems. However, since we did not have the opportunity to intervene, we made plans for their hospitalisation, which was still good. This indicates that we must create a support system that can help these people using the community relationship before it is too late. Furthermore, it is an excellent opportunity for us to break through all the barriers and to come forward and intervene more quickly and effectively.

Piyumanthi: I would like to take this opportunity to add a small addition to his statement. As he mentioned, there is a high tendency for suicide among university students. However, this also exists in institutions. Based on my observations, many people struggle with depression, even in the institution where I work and among those who hold high positions. This sometimes leads to attempted suicides. Other reasons include the economic crisis, pressure of the positions and the fact that they do not talk about their feelings with others.

I remember an officer who was greatly appreciated within the institution and at the national level. However, suddenly his performance decreased significantly without any reason. Thus, I intervened when the head of the institution was taking disciplinary action against him due to their lack of knowledge about his situation. Specifically, I said: 'Let us look into this a bit more because he has been working well. Let us find out why his performance has decreased'. We eventually found that he was dealing with a personal problem at home. In this case, if we did not intervene, it could have resulted in depression and possible suicide.

I must emphasise that in today's complex social system, everyone is somewhat affected by the economic crisis. In some cases, people become isolated and lack an effective emotional support system. Therefore, it is important to further discuss this in light of social work practitioners.

Rethinking traditional concepts, practices and systems

Michelle: During my community work, a typical traditional word that came to mind was *kayiya* (කයිය). Usually, when we say *kayiya* we mean 'speaking'. Furthermore, it can mean 'social capital'. You must have heard the word *goyam kayiya* (ගොයම් කයිය). This is when people want to harvest their paddy fields, after which they go to the village, give *betel* and mobilise the people. In this case, the work is based on mutual trust and recognition. If they had mental or economic problems, they simply spoke to the head person, who made the necessary arrangements. Since our society is based on a traditional social work system and an economy related to farming, recreating effective systems such as *goyam kayiya* is essential.

Female 2: I have a quick addition. I am not sure that you would agree, but we have a concept called *ḷinda ḷanga samgamaya* (ළිඳ ළඟ සංගමය) in the past. Specifically, when women gathered to collect water or bathe, they discussed their domestic beliefs or any problems they were experiencing. In other words, they had some type of relief. I recently found a similar system in my community, where women gathered and gossiped. However, due to the COVID-19 pandemic, they stopped this practice and had no other way to express their emotions.

Tharindu Kasunpriya: I do not know the traditional word for this, but there was something called 'leadership in villages'. In the past, people in the villages had someone who was responsible for writing letters. In times of need, this person wrote letters to other people in the community, after which the people responded to provide support. In this case, someone provided the badly needed funds when money was urgently needed. We used to have this type of practice in which the community was strengthened by the actions of such leaders. Perhaps we can reintroduce such a system in today's communities to identify the gaps in society and use them for the practice of social work.

Male 2: In today's society, there are many unions and societies such as the Elders' Society, the Children's Society, the Women's Society, the Village Development Society, the Death Aid Society and the Water Society. These societies have been established for various purposes. However, there are no regulations or coordination in place. Perhaps as social workers, we can help create the necessary regulations or coordinate their services for better community development.

Rathnayake: I can add a little more to this discussion. Regarding the lack of an effective support system, we used to have an effective support system in which people could talk about anything. However, such systems have disappeared due to technological adaptations and/or the generation gap. For example, children's interactions with their parents have decreased dramatically due to technological devices. Meanwhile, parents do not necessarily interact with their children for the same reason. Thus, it would be helpful for them to talk to social workers and professionals about self-coping mechanisms.

When I was working in Bangalore, India, it was a very technological city. However, some people participated in something called 'laughter yoga', in which they would deliberately laugh as a form of mental and physical release. Perhaps with social work intervention, we can re-introduce similar activities that do not include technical devices.

I agree that *ḷinda ḷanga saṃgamaya*, which was mentioned earlier, can be good for society. Specifically, talking about problems with others is extremely important among the elderly, who are becoming increasingly isolated. When we look at the younger generation, they are also becoming isolated, which has increased their dropout rates and suicidal tendencies.

I know this, especially as someone who works with young people. Therefore, I believe that it is important to have further discussions on this matter, especially in the Sri Lankan context.

Male 3: Many people know the term *gami diriya; Gami* means 'villages' and *diriya* means 'encourage'. In the past, empowerment of people occurred through this concept, which was well known for its contribution of labour and ideas to community development. Perhaps such an approach can be suggested for rural development today.

Challenges in a changing society

Male 3: Furthermore, I have a question for Ms Piyumanthi. Since my field of interest is research, you mentioned that loneliness among the elderly had been identified as a social problem by the *Grama Niladhari* divisions. Are there any reasons for this?

Piyumanthi: The main reason is the change in our family system. Imagine a mother and father with their daughter, son and/or grandchildren. In this situation and in an economy, we cannot necessarily take care of the elderly. Meanwhile, the walls around the houses have further exacerbated the situation by preventing people from easily visiting their neighbours.

Let me give one example. The mother leaves the house and talks to her neighbour when the children go to work or school. However, children do not want their privacy compromised when they are home. Thus, the mother does not leave and isolates herself. Over time, her mental condition deteriorates. I observed this after coming to my division of the University of Colombo and conducting a two-day research project. At the end of this project, I realised that all the elderly in the community were unhappy, since they had no one to talk to about their problems. Therefore, I proposed having daycare centres for the elderly, similar to those for children. There is no place like the village environment. However, the problem of loneliness remains in this population.

Male 4: In the global crisis, the youth left the country primarily and the elderly became isolated and lonely, which will continue to happen.

Chamara Kumarasinghe: In the past, we told children stories. When there were power outages, we turned off our phones, after which the grandparents would tell stories in the dark. In other instances, we played folk games, such as *mallawapora* and *porapol*, with other villagers. However, over time, this was limited to one or two small games. Look at what our children are doing today. They only play individual games, not team-based games. Therefore, we must re-examine how we lost this tradition and determine how we can talk with our children and focus on their well-being and mental state. Such approaches could perhaps reduce our problems in society.

Male 4: I want to add something to this discussion about the elderly. Some people were in prominent positions in their work lives. However, after retirement, they suddenly lack the recognition and interactions that they once had daily. In this regard, perhaps they could use their time to work as consultants in an established centre/organisation. Meanwhile, the younger generation can come to them and share their experiences. I believe it would be good to create such opportunities for this population.

Follow Up

Q1. What are the key terms of your social work practices in a specific context, without necessarily using English terms?

Ranaweera: Let us wrap up with a quick discussion on three questions. Regarding the first question, what are the critical terms of social work practice in a specific context, without using English terms? Based on your presentations, I understand that you have been educated at the NISD. Therefore, your views are perhaps based on modern, Westernised social work theories and practices. Meanwhile, whatever term you use is invariably connected with English terms. To my knowledge, the Sinhala words are *shramadaana* (ශ්‍රමදාන), *kayiya* (කයිය), *depayin nagi sitima* (දෙපයින් නැගී සිටීම), *svadhinava jīvat vima* (ස්වාධීනව ජීවත් වීම) and *anunta atanopaa jivat vima* (අනුන්ට අතනොපා ජීවත් වීම). Are there any other words? Maybe there are *sajivikaranaya* (සජීවිකරණය) and *konda kelin tiyaganima* (කොන්ද කෙලින් තියාගැනීම). Even if this is true, we are paradoxically thinking in the context of social work. In other words, offering assistance is not considered social work. Is finding ways for people to become more independent and empowered than social work?

Female 3: I have carried out some projects using different approaches. It has worked well in the province.

Ranaweera: Yes. Our connection with Sri Lanka is strong. For example, when

I say that I am sick, my relatives are the first to arrive, followed by my friends and other locals. They come and ask if they can help and offer support. Does this not happen in social work? Where did the word 'social' come from and what is its origin? We must look at this perspective since society, especially the village level, has rapidly changed. For example, there are no such groups in the village. Even for *shramadaana*, finding people can be difficult. Meanwhile, people participating in the Death Society expect to be paid for their work.

Male 6: I remember when a man would clean the road to the temple for certain religious events or funerals. Even when it rained and the road was covered with sand, he still cleaned it, removing every leaf or branch. We called people like him 'social workers'.

Ranaweera: Yes, there is no such thing now. When a funeral is held, the order is given to the florist shop, the coffin is taken and speeches are not necessarily given. These are the changes in society. However, some remote villages still adhere to previous traditions.

Q2. Why do you think these perspectives are essential?

Ranaweera: Regarding the second question, why do you think it is worthwhile to include the beliefs and values of society in social work? Now, we will talk about indigenous practices. Do we have an indigenous practice like that?

If you look at people with disabilities, most are cared for at home. This is the same for children. However, despite the efforts of the government and other welfare services, some people do not want to use their services based on their beliefs and values. So, again, why do you think including your beliefs and values in social work is important?

Ashker: We have yet to convert to the Western system, even though we apply such thinking at the local level. Thus, we must find ways to apply the beliefs and values of individuals, while utilising English terminology and approaches.

Female 5: The other thing is that, even if we consider this nature-nurture concept, which is Western-based, we still need to influence our culture and environment. In this regard, it is important to include indigenous schools.

Male 7: I believe it also has a religious influence. For example, social work must integrate the concept of merits in society. In fact, in many villages, people work according to this concept. Even if a canal is dug or unwanted branches are cut from a tree, they believe that such work is meritorious. However, when we practice social work without considering religious influences, problems may arise and long-term sustainability is compromised. Moreover, if we simply apply Western-rooted concepts, then additional problems may arise. Therefore, including such beliefs and values is essential for the local people.

Chamra Kumansinghe: We still accept concepts such as 'I', 'we' (*api*) 'our' (*ape*) family, 'our' school and 'our' village. With that, we are still not moving away from them. If we continue to talk about them, then we need to improve them. It is important to do these things.

Q3. What do you think about the roots of these terms/ perspectives? (e.g. the West, home country or others?)

Ranaweera: Let us go to the final questions. What do you think about the roots of practical perspectives? Is our approach based on Western thinking, the Sri Lankan perspective or a mixture? To what extent are these views and terms recognised among social workers in other countries or in Sri Lanka? Do other people have an idea? Are people involved in other social services aware of social work?

Ashker: In Sri Lanka, people use their levels of authority and influence from different perspectives, which is sometimes highly polarising. You see this among counsellors, psychiatrists, doctors or whoever provides psychiatric/ clinical social work. As stated earlier, this has resulted in welfare resentment and free liberalism among some community members. Even right now, we are practicing whether this is true.

Regarding the second part of the question, we must apply a mixture of Western thinking that applies theories and scientific methods and an approach based on Sri Lankan religious and traditional influences. In this way, the social work profession in Sri Lanka can be officially recognised globally while still focusing on values and beliefs at the local level. However, we can only do this in our culture. This has also happened in the US and the UK. Eventually, social workers in their countries were recognised as professional social workers.

Closing remarks

Ranaweera: Thank you. I want to close by emphasising that we will continue to explore new avenues of social work practice in Sri Lanka. Although we have been teaching and following Western-rooted techniques, we acknowledge that there are many social workers in Sri Lanka. In fact, UNICEF refers to it as 'the social service workforce'.

In 2014, when I was retiring from the NISD, I saw that the government was planning to appoint 40,000 graduates as social service officers and development officers. Interestingly, they were not officially called 'social workers', although they were trained to perform such work at both the community and the village levels. Even when I was teaching the introduction to social work, the first lesson was about how social work helps people. In this sense, the definition of social work is very complex. However, considering the following question is important: How do we, as social workers, continue to provide support and assistance for those in need while considering the religious and traditional beliefs of those we serve? We have fundamental beliefs about *Metta*, *Karana* and *Muditha*. In Hinduism, the same similar beliefs exist. However, these values are within us. Therefore, we must remember this and consider how it can be incorporated into the definition of social work in Sri Lanka.

Appendix

Abstracts of Research-Based Presentations

Psycho-social Challenges in Active Participation of Students with Disabilities in Vocational Education

M.S. Shifna
Bachelor of Social Work Student
National Institute of Social Development

T. Tharshan
National Institute of Social Development

Abstract: This study examined psycho-social challenges in the active participation of students with disabilities in vocational education. It used a qualitative design to analyse a sample of differently abled students, staff, graduated students and parents at the Seeduwa Vocational Training Institution. Data were collected through key informant interviews, observations and a case study. Thus, eight differently abled students were selected for the interviews, while eight people (two teachers, one director, one warden, two parents and two graduated students) were primary data givers. As for the case study, the data were analysed through thematic analysis. The finding revealed that the students experienced various difficulties, including poor concentration, anxiety and lack of interest, motivation, resources, counselling and institutional facilities and effective classroom management, all of which affected their active participation in vocational education. Meanwhile, other challenges related to the educational environment in terms of the use of technological teaching aids and the inclusion of an appropriate number of students in the class. The implication of the findings is that teachers must understand the psychological and physical capacities of students with disabilities to improve their participation and motivation in vocational education.

Keywords: Active participation, Differently abled, Vocational education, Psycho-social challenges

Potential of Adaptive Dance Classes as a Strength-based Social Work Approach for Enhancing the Social Skills of Individuals with Special Needs

Varuni Michelle Fernando
Department of Medical Humanities,
Faculty of Medicine, University of Colombo

Abstract: This study examined the potential of adaptive dance classes as a strength-based social work approach to improve social skills of people with special needs. Therefore, the researcher, a social work student and Visharadh from Bharatanatyam, conducted this study at the Kosala Dullewa Foundation for Special Needs in Colombo, focusing on individuals with Down syndrome aged 11–32 years. The sample comprised 15 participants, including five students, one parent for each student, the founder of the institution, two dance mentors and three dance volunteers without special needs. Furthermore, this study used case studies, in-depth interviews and participant observations to collect data on the marginalisation of individuals with special needs in Sri Lanka. Based on the findings, adaptive dance classes are a promising intervention to promote social inclusion of students and have successfully tapped into their hidden potential by teaching them various dance styles such as subtle movements, creative dance, Kandyan dance and Bharatanatyam. Moreover, it was instrumental in enhancing the social skills of the students, leveraging a wide range of strengths that encompassed material strengths such as incorporating music, having a class to practice and having a stage to perform on and sponsorships. Meanwhile, dance mentors used various techniques to cultivate students' social skills, such as mirroring, imitation and collaborative dance, which helped them express themselves. The implication of the findings is that this approach can promote both primary and secondary socialisation and promote superior social skills in those who have mastered subtle dance movements over complex ones. Regarding the methodologies, unlike traditional teaching methods, adaptive dance classes can identify and mobilise the resources and skills that the user possesses, rather than focus on the root cause of the problem. In summary, adaptive dance classes in the Sri Lankan context can be a valuable contribution to the social work profession, as they offer a disability-inclusive environment that promotes social inclusion for individuals with special needs.

Keywords: Adaptive Dance Classes, Social Skills, Social Inclusion

Improving the Fine Motor Skills of Children with Difficulties in Pre-Writing Activities

Thahir Noorul Isra
Department of Inclusive Education,
National Institute of Education

Abstract: The purpose of this study was to focus on improving the fine motor skills of children with difficulties in pre-writing activities. In this regard, this study conducted observations, interviews and document studies using an action research design in which qualitative and quantitative data were collected. The sample of this study included one child (selected from five children) who participated in the identification process in the Department of Inclusive Education at the National Institute of Education. Specifically, we examined the fine motor skills of the fingers of this student with special needs (i.e. Down syndrome), who was ready to enter grade one in the inclusive education classroom but was experiencing difficulties in pre-writing activities. However, through continuous practice, the student's fine motor skills improved significantly and it became easier to achieve certain goals based on the different teacher's pedagogical methods.

Keywords: இயக்க திறன், விடய ஆய்வு, முன் எழுத்து பயிற்சி, டவுன்ஸ் சின்றம் (Fine motor skills, Pre-writing activities, Down syndrome)

Children with Disabilities: Ensuring Disability-Inclusive Education in the Estate Sector in Sri Lanka

Muhammad Ashker
National Institute of Social Development

Jeyaruban Varatharajah
National Institute of Social Development

Abstract: Educational accessibility for children with disabilities is one of the most important rights recognised by the CRPD, the ICCPR and the ICESCR. Meanwhile, prejudice, myths and lack of pregnancy awareness are the most crucial issues among the estate sector in relation to children with disabilities. Thus, this study explored several issues related to disability-inclusive education in the context of stigmas, myths and malpractices related to disability and childbirth in Sri Lanka. Previous research has shown that the lack of accessibility and relevant assistive technology has inhibited children with disabilities from participating in education and related activities. For example, children with hearing impairment have been intentionally (or unintentionally) discriminated due to the lack of appropriate facilities, which has resulted in higher dropout rates (ESJW, Vol: 6 (2) 2022). However, it should be noted that children with disabilities either never attended school or dropped out due to myths about disabilities, child labour, segregation, stigma, inaccessibility, discrimination and internal migration. In this study, we focused on a sample of 45 children with disabilities in the estate sector, nine of whom we aimed to eliminate the myths related to hearing impairment, semi-visual impairment, hearing and speaking impairment, hyperactivity, physical impairment and Down syndrome. For example, one myth was that children are born with disabilities, due to the sins of their parents. In this regard, reinforcement and cognitive behavioural modifications can be effective psycho-therapeutic interventions for such students.

116

Keywords: Children with disabilities, Disability-inclusive education, Myths, Interventions

Social Work with Indigenous Communities (Veddas) in Sri Lanka: Perspectives on Educational Preparation and Practice

Thilina Yasith Kekulandala
Flinders University, South Australia

Nilupuli Nayanathara Jayathilaka
National Institute of Social Development

Abstract: This qualitative case study examined the challenges experienced by the Vedda community (an indigenous group in Sri Lanka) and investigated diverse perspectives on the preparation of educational programmes and the practice of social work to meet their needs. The rich cultural heritage and traditional way of life of the Veddas are deeply rooted in their forest-dependent lifestyle and spiritual beliefs. However, they are currently facing numerous obstacles, such as land encroachment, marginalisation and cultural deterioration, endangering their continued existence as a distinct community. Therefore, this study demonstrated that while social work in Australia incorporates numerous aspects of society, the Sri Lankan context remains relatively underdeveloped and lacks a holistic approach, particularly in terms of indigenous populations. Furthermore, this study included multiple goals: promoting the inclusion of indigenous social work in the fundamental curriculum of social work education, suggesting effective methods for social work students to learn about working with indigenous communities (e.g. establishing connections, engaging in consultations and participating in field- and evidence-based education) and determining the knowledge and abilities that social workers need to effectively engage with indigenous communities such as the Vedda community. The findings of this study will contribute to the development of social work practices that are culturally sensitive and tailored to the specific needs of indigenous communities. Furthermore, this study can promote the sustainability of social work in Sri Lanka and the preservation of Vedda culture and heritage by shedding light on the challenges they face and the necessary preparations in educational programmes of social workers.

Keywords: Veddas community, Indigenous social work, Sri Lanka; වැද්දන්, ආදිවාසීන් පිළිබඳ සමාජ වැඩ, ශ්‍රී ලංකාව

Conference Timetable on 2 November 2023

Opening	Coordinator: Muhammad Ashker
Noriko Totsuka	Opening Remarks

Keynotes

Amarawansa Ranaweera	Significance and Challenges of Sharing Experiences in Social Work Practices
Shamini Attanayake	Volunteerism and Social Work

Concurrent Session 1 (Practice-oriented)	Coordinator: Masateru Higashida and Amarawansa Ranaweera
E.A. Upeksha Piyumanthi	692, කුණ්ඩසාලේ දකුණ ග්‍රාමනිලධාරී කොට්ඨාශයේ සමාජ වැඩ වෘත්තිමය ප්‍රවේශ භාවිතය පිළිබඳව කෙටි විමසුමක්
K.H. Chamara Kumarasinghe	උපතින් ආබාධ සහිත (කායික හෝ මානසික) අවුරුදු පහට අඩු දරුවන්ගේ අනාගත සුරක්ෂිතභාවය වෙනුවෙන් එම දෙමව්පියන් මානසික හා ආර්ථිකව ශක්තිමත් කිරීම
Chandima Jayasena and S.P. Tharindu Kasunpriya	Fostering Inter-ethnic Understanding Through the Sinhala and Tamil New Year Practice in Sri Lankan Preschools
R.M.H. Yasintha Rathnayake	Youth Empowerment Through Volunteer-based Community Development
Varathagowry Vasudevan	Harnessing and Optimising Fieldwork Through Indigenous Supervision: A Reflective and Reflexive Approach

120

Concurrent Session 2 Coordinator/Commentator: Jeyaruban
Varatharajah and Muhammad Ashker

Varuni Michelle Fernando	The Potential of Adaptive Dance Classes as a Strength-based Social Work Approach to Enhancing the Social Skills of Individuals with Special Needs
Thahir Noorul Isra	Improving the Fine Motor Skills of Children with Difficulties in Pre-writing Activities
M.S. Shifna and T. Tharshan	Psycho-social Challenges in the Active Participation of Students with Disabilities in Vocational Education
Thilina Yasith Kekulandala and Nilupuli Nayanathara	Social Work with Indigenous Communities (Veddas) in Sri Lanka: Perspectives on Educational Preparation and Practice
Vivetha Gunaretnam	Incorporating Social Case Work Practice: Enhancing Individual Well-being Through Comprehensive Support in the Sri Lankan Context
Muhammad Ashker and Jeyaruban Varatharajah	Children with Disabilities: Ensuring Disability-inclusive Education in the Estate Sector in Sri Lanka

Dialogue Coordinator/Commentator:
(Main Session) Higashida and Ranaweera

Participants	Dialogue with Practitioners
Masateru Higashida	A Framework for Dialogue: Why Do We Focus on Local and Foreign Knowledge in Social Work Practice?

References

Akimoto, T. (2004). The essence of international social work and nine world maps: How to induct students into the secrets of ISW. *Social Welfare*. Japan Women's University, *45*, 1–15.

Akimoto, T. (2015). あなたは世界定義を受け入れられるか?:『専門職ソーシャルワークでないソーシャルワーク』を例に. *Studies on Social Work*, *41*(3), 187–198 (in Japanese).

Akimoto, T. (2017). The globalization of Western-rooted professional social work and exploration of Buddhist social work. In T. Akimoto (Ed.), *From western-rooted professional social work to Buddhist social work: Exploring Buddhist social work* (pp. 1–41). Gakubunsha.

Akimoto, T. (2020) [Preface]. Buddhist social work in Sri Lanka: Past and present. In T. Akimoto et al. (Eds.), *Gakubunsha* (pp. vi–viii).

Akimoto, T. (2024). *International social work of all people in the whole world: A new construction*. Junposha.

Akimoto, T., Fujimori, Y., Gohori, J., & Matsuo, K. (2020). Objection to Western-rooted professional social work: To make social work something truly of the world: Indigenization is not the answer. In J. Gohori (Ed.), *The journey of Buddhist social work: Exploring the potential of Buddhism in Asian social work* (pp. 62–69). Asian Research Institute for International Social Work.

Asian Research Institute for International Social Work. (2018). Working definition and current curricula of Buddhist social work. In T. Akimoto & M. Hattori (Eds.), *Working definition and current curricula of Buddhist social work: Hanoi international expert meeting*. VNU University of Social Sciences & Humanities and ARIISW, Shukutoku University.

Barker, R. L. (1999). *The social work dictionary, 4th edition*. NASW Press.

Cooper, J. E. (2007). Strengthening the case for community-based learning in teacher education. *Journal of Teacher Education*, *58*(3), 245–255. https://doi.org/10.1177/0022487107299979

Department of Census and Statistics. (2012). *Census of population and housing 2011* [Final report]. Department of Census and Statistics. http://www.statistics.gov.lk/Population/StaticalInformation/CPH2011/CensusPopulationHousing2012-FinalReport.

Dominelli, L. (2012). Globalisation and indigenisation: Reconciling the irreconcilable in social work. In K. H. Lyons, M. Pawar, T. Hokenstad, & N. Hall (Eds.), *The SAGE handbook of international social work* (pp. 39–55). SAGE.

Gray, M., & Coates, J. (2010). From "indigenization" to cultural relevance. In M. Gray, J. Coates, & M. Yellow Bird (Eds.), *Indigenous social work around the world: Towards culturally relevant education and practice* (pp. 13–30). Routledge.

122

Higashida, M. (2015). Role of the overseas social worker in community-based rehabilitation in Sri Lanka: JICA volunteers' practice in a rural area. *Journal of International Health*, 77–86 (in Japanese).

Higashida, M. (2016). Integration of religion and spirituality with social work practice in disability issues: Participant observation in a rural area of Sri Lanka. *SAGE Open*, *6*(1). https://doi.org/10.1177/2158244015627672

Higashida, M. (2023a). Education and training opportunities for local and indigenous social workers: Case studies in disability-related fields from an international development perspective. *Social Work Education*, *42*(4), 548–565. https://doi.org/1 0.1080/02615479.2021.1978966

Higashida, M. (2023c). 国際開発ソーシャルワーク入門 改訂版. Osaka Metropolitan University Press. (in Japanese).

Higashida, M. (2024). Process of constructing alternative social work discourses in Asia: A case study of Buddhist social work as social representations. *Asian Social Work and Policy Review*, *18*(1). https://doi.org/10.1111/aswp.12298

Higashida, M., Ranaweera, A., & Herath, C. (2022). Exploring the social representations of social work in the Sri Lankan cultural context: A qualitative study. *Sustainability*, *14*(23), 16197. https://doi.org/10.3390/su142316197

IASSW, & International Federation of Social Workers. (2020). *The global standard for social work education and training*. International Association of School of Social Work and International Federation of Social Workers.

International Federation of Social Workers, & IASSW. (2014). Global definition of the social work profession. https://www.ifsw.org/what-is-social-work/global-definition-of-social-work/

International Labour Organization. (2020). Opportunities and challenges in formation and functioning of trade unions in Sri Lanka. ILO Country Office for Sri Lanka and the Maldives. https://www.ilo.org/wcmsp5/groups/public/---asia/---ro-bangkok/---ilo-colombo/documents/publication/wcms_735679.pdf.

Kolb, D. A., Boyatzis, R. E., & Mainemelis, C. (2014). Experiential learning theory: Previous research and new directions. In *Perspectives on thinking, learning, and cognitive styles* (pp. 227–247). Routledge.

Liyanage, C. (2017). Sociocultural construction of disability in Sri Lanka: Charity to rights-based approach. In S. Halder, & L.C. Assaf (Eds.), *Inclusion, disability and culture: An ethnographic perspective traversing abilities and challenges* (pp.251–265). Cham: Springer.

Midgley, J. (2016). Promoting reciprocal international social work exchanges: Professional imperialism revisited. In M. Gray, J. Coates, & M. Y. Bird (Eds.), *Indigenous social work around the world* (pp. 31–45). Routledge.

Mishima, A. (2016). The transition of knowledge in the definition of social work: What is "indigenous knowledge"? *Japanese Journal of Social Welfare*, *57*(1), 113–124 (in

Japanese).

Noyoo, N., & Kleibl, T. (2019). Setting the scene for critical new social work approaches in the neoliberal postcolonial era. In T. Kleibl, R. Lutz, N. Noyoo, B. Bunk, A. Dittmann, & B. Seepamore (Eds.), *The Routledge handbook of postcolonial social work* (pp. 1–8). Routledge.

Offer, J. (2006). *An intellectual history of British social policy: Idealism versus non-idealism*. Policy Press.

Payne, M., & Askeland, G. A. (2016). *Globalization and international social work: Postmodern change and challenge*. Routledge.

Perera, M. (1991). The impact of macro-events on social structure in Sri Lanka. In E. Masini & S. Stratigos (Eds.), *Women, households and change* (pp. 80–150). United Nations University Press.

Ranaweera, A. (2013). *Review and record of the history of social work education in Sri Lanka*. National Institute of Social Development.

Razick, A. S. (2017). *Socio cultural issues and the relationships between Buddhists and Muslims in Sri Lanka*. Faculty of Islamic Studies and Arabic Language, South Eastern University of Sri Lanka.

Rowe, S., Baldry, E., & Earles, W. (2015). Decolonising social work research: Learning from critical indigenous approaches. *Australian Social Work*, *68*(3), 296–308. https://doi.org/10.1080/0312407X.2015.1024264

Samaraweera, H. U. S. (2020). Social work education in contemporary Sri Lanka: Issues and challenges. In S. M. Sajid, R. Baikady, C. Sheng-Li, & H. Sakaguchi (Eds.), *The Palgrave handbook of global social work education* (pp. 379–391). Springer.

Shamila, S. (2020). Impediments to professionalising social work education in Sri Lanka. In S. M. Sajid, R. Baikady, C. Sheng-Li, & H. Sakaguchi (Eds.), *The Palgrave handbook of global social work education* (pp. 671–688). Springer.

Shardlow, S., & Doel, M. (1996). Practice learning and teaching. *Practice Learning and Teaching*, 1–216.

Somananda, O. (2020). Understanding of Sri Lankan society as a premise to understand the Buddhist "social work". In T. Akimoto (Ed.), *Buddhist social work in Sri Lanka: Past and present* (pp. 3–25). Gakubunsha.

Stellar, J. E., & Keltner, D. (2014). Compassion. In *Handbook of positive emotions* (pp. 329–341). Guilford Press.

Tsui, M. S. (2004). Supervision models in social work: From nature to culture. *Asian Journal of Counselling*.

Twikirize, M., & Spitzer, H. (2019). *Social work practice in Africa: Indigenous and innovative approaches*. Fountain Publishers.

Unnathi, H., & Samaraweera, S. (2024). Cultural sensitivity and social work within the multicultural landscape of Sri Lanka. In J. Przeperski, & R. Baikady. (Eds.), *The Routledge international handbook of social work teaching* (pp. 519-530).

124

Routledge.
Uyangoda, J. (2005). Ethnic conflict, the state and the tsunami disaster in Sri Lanka. *Inter-Asia Cultural Studies*, *6*(3), 341–352. https://doi.org/10.1080/14649370500169979
Wickramasinghe, A. (2020). Definition of Buddhist social work. In T. Akimoto (Ed.), *Buddhist social work in Sri Lanka: Past and present* (pp. 131–151). Gakubunsha.
Wickramasinghe, A., Kodituwakku, C., & Perera, J. (2020). Data collection as a prerequisite for curriculum design of Buddhist social work higher education: Practice based research. In T. Akimoto (Ed.), *Buddhist social work in Sri Lanka: Past and present* (pp. 54–89). Gakubunsha.

Index

126

F

Faculty Development 11

Family x, 10, 13, 18, 32, 38, 39, 45, 48, 50, 51, 52, 53, 54, 55, 67, 73, 74, 76, 77, 78, 79, 83, 84, 95, 96, 100, 104, 107

Foreign knowledge viii, xi, 91

G

Gami diriya 104

Genogram 74, 75

Global Definition of the Social Work Profession vii, 18, 25, 31, 101

Globalisation xi, 87

Global North 83

Grama Niladhari xi, 45, 46, 48, 52, 53, 97, 104

H

Hindu 60

Horoscope 76, 78, 79

Human rights 74

I

Imposition 92

India 58, 67, 84, 100, 103

Indigenous peoples 117

Indigenous practice and knowledge vii, viii, ix, x, 17, 24, 32, 33, 81, 82, 85, 91, 95, 98, 101, 106

Indigenous social work ix, 24, 32, 33, 86, 117

Indigenous supervision xi, 82

Injustice 31

Inter-ethnic understanding 60

International Association of Schools of Social Work (IASSW) 18, 25, 83, 101

International Federation of Social Workers (IFSW) 18, 25, 83, 101

Internationalisation 24

International Non-governmental Organisation (INGO) 57, 58, 59

International perspective viii

International social work 18

Islam ix, 100

J

Japan International Cooperation Agency (JICA) 37, 38

Jennings Report 18, 25

Justice 32

K

Kandy 46, 57, 59

Kayiya 98, 102, 105

Kegalle 57, 59, 60

L

Leadership 46, 68, 70, 74, 103

M

Marginalisation 38, 42, 45, 99, 112, 117

Master of Social Work (MSW) 12, 46, 52, 58, 66, 67, 74, 83

Medical Officers of Health (MOH) 52, 98

Mental health 12, 51, 67, 68, 101

Metta 108

Mutuality x, 18, 58, 81, 102

N

Narratives 22

National Institute of Social Development (NISD) vii, x, 11, 12, 13, 22, 25, 33, 52, 58, 61, 62, 66, 67, 74, 83, 85, 94, 105, 108

Non-governmental Organisation (NGO) xi, 57, 58, 74

大阪公立大学出版会（OMUP）とは
本出版会は、大阪の5公立大学－大阪市立大学、大阪府立大学、大阪女子大学、大阪
府立看護大学、大阪府立看護大学医療技術短期大学部－の教授を中心に2001年に設立
された大阪公立大学共同出版会を母体としています。2005年に大阪府立の4大学が統
合されたことにより、公立大学は大阪府立大学と大阪市立大学のみになり、2022年に
その両大学が統合され、大阪公立大学となりました。これを機に、本出版会は大阪公
立大学出版会（Osaka Metropolitan University Press「略称：OMUP」）と名称を改め、
現在に至っています。なお、本出版会は、2006年から特定非営利活動法人（NPO）と
して活動しています。

About Osaka Metropolitan University Press (OMUP)
Osaka Metropolitan University Press was originally named Osaka Municipal
Universities Press and was founded in 2001 by professors from Osaka City
University, Osaka Prefecture University, Osaka Women's University, Osaka
Prefectural College of Nursing, and Osaka Prefectural Medical Technology College.
Four of these universities later merged in 2005, and a further merger with Osaka
City University in 2022 resulted in the newly-established Osaka Metropolitan
University. On this occasion, Osaka Municipal Universities Press was renamed to
Osaka Metropolitan University Press (OMUP). OMUP has been recognized as a
Non-Profit Organization (NPO) since 2006.

Exploring Alternative Social Work Knowledge

Based on the Narratives of Practitioners from Sri Lanka

2024年7月1日　発行

編著者　東田全央、M.T.R. Shamini Attanayake、
　　　　Amarawansa Ranaweera、Muhammad Ashker
発行者　八木孝司
発行所　大阪公立大学出版会（OMUP）
　　　　〒599-8531　大阪府堺市中区学園町1－1
　　　　大阪公立大学内
　　　　TEL　072(251)6533
　　　　FAX　072(254)9539
印刷所　石川特殊特急製本株式会社

ISBN 978－4－909933－76－8